AF664381

How to
Manage Meetings

THE SUNDAY TIMES

CREATING SUCCESS

How to Manage Meetings

Alan Barker

KOGAN PAGE

Publisher's Note

Every possible effort has been made to ensure that the information contained in this book is accurate at the time of going to press, and the publishers and authors cannot accept responsibility for any errors or omissions, however caused. No responsibility for loss or damage occasioned to any person acting, or refraining from action, as a result of the material in this publication can be accepted by the editor, the publisher or any of the authors.

First South Asian Edition 2007
Reprinted 2008, 2009

Kogan Page India Private Limited
4737/23 Ansari Road,
Daryaganj
New Delhi 110 002

This edition is for sale in the Indian subcontinent only. Not for export elsewhere.

ISBN-10: 81-7554-323-X
ISBN-13: 978-81-7554-323-2

Published by Vinod Vasishtha for Kogan Page India Private Limited,
4737/23 Ansari Road, Daryaganj, New Delhi - 110 002.

Printed and bound at Raj Press, R-3, Inderpuri, New Delhi - 110 012

Contents

Introduction

The great economist J K Galbraith once remarked: 'Meetings are indispensable when you don't want to do anything.'

Most of us have horror stories of meetings we have been forced to endure. And yet, with most people working in organisations spending 60 per cent of their time in meetings, such dry humour is no longer adequate. We *must* improve the way we manage meetings – and urgently.

We can forget why we hold meetings. The sheer habit of calling them can blind us to the need for clear objectives. Meetings should help us get results: they are a mechanism for achieving action in our organisations. Chapter 1 looks at what meetings are, why we hold them (and why we *should* hold them!) and the golden rules that apply to every meeting. Chapter 9 is a reminder of what needs to happen *after* a meeting, to ensure that it has effective outcomes and has not been a waste of time.

Managing a meeting is a key managerial skill. Meetings are where managers are most clearly visible as managers, and where leaders can be seen to lead. Chairing a meeting gives us the opportunity to make a real impact: on our team, our colleagues, our customers, and on our own managers. Chapters 3 and 5 both look at the responsibilities of chairing.

But participants also have a role in managing meetings. To

participate – fully and positively – means more than making your voice heard and getting your point across. It means taking a full part in the group conversation: helping others to make their points well, encouraging and guiding, listening and responding appropriately. Chapter 7 looks at the varied skills we all need to improve the way we participate in meetings.

Using the drills well – the agenda, the minutes, the elements of formal control – is obviously important. Chapter 4 contains all you need to know to use these common drills of management meetings effectively. But meetings rely for their success also on more intangible elements: the shifting web of relationships within a group, the complicated cut and thrust of conversation. These are less easy to manage; but if we can control them, the meeting has a greater chance of being productive.

A meeting is a group of people thinking together. That is why we need to know how groups work, and how we think in groups. Chapter 2 explores the way groups behave. The complexities of group dynamics can be daunting – that's why I've added a summary of the chapter's main ideas at its conclusion. But I make no apology for including this material. If we can understand something of how groups operate, we will be better prepared to participate as a group member at our next meeting. Chapter 6 considers conversation: the subtleties of speaking and listening, the signals that we need to read to understand how a conversation is developing, and the techniques we can call on to make our conversations more disciplined.

Most meetings involve solving problems of some kind. Chapter 8 looks at problem solving. The format of the meeting may vary, according to the kind of problem we are tackling. Chapter 10 explores various meeting formats, including negotiation and brainstorming, as well as some thoughts on international meetings and meetings held as conference calls or video links.

We're all responsible for the success of the meetings we attend. Whether as a Chair, a participant, or a minute-taker, we can all find ways to manage meetings better. If you are frustrated at the waste of time, effort and energy in your organisation's meetings – and if you want to do something about it – then this book is for you.

1

What is a meeting?

Meetings are at the very heart of management.

It is in meetings that we make the key decisions that shape our future actions and the future of our organisations. And as life at work becomes ever more complicated, there's every reason to think that we shall be holding more meetings in the future. The rise of teamwork alone is a key factor. Teams need regular meetings to maintain their identity, to understand what they have to do and help them find their place in the wider organisation. In addition, many of our meetings are with people we may not know well: project team members, clients or suppliers, consultants and contractors. We need to be able to work together quickly, with minimal introductions. Others are held at a distance, using telephone, video or computer links. Of course, the more traditional types of meeting – the committee, the team briefing, the board meeting – are unlikely to disappear.

But other developments in the way we work are responsible for an increase in the number of meetings in our diaries. These include:

- project management;
- cross-functional teams;
- self-managed teams;

- outsourcing and increasingly complex partnerships;
- internal market relationships;
- increasing numbers of associates and contract workers;
- the growth in consultancy, both external and internal;
- networking within and between divisions of increasingly global corporations.

Yet the complaint arises, over and over again, that most business meetings are a waste of time. What is going wrong? Let's begin by asking the most basic question: what are meetings for?

A group thinking together

Here, for starters, is a brief definition of a meeting:

> A meeting is a group of people thinking purposefully together.

This simple definition distinguishes meetings from interviews – where the conversation is led by one person and focused on another – and from casual conversations in the pub or the company restaurant. Let's briefly examine the key elements of this definition.

First, a meeting involves a group of people. To be sure, we attend meetings as individuals; but we also behave as members of a group. Our behaviour in the meeting will be affected by our relationship to the group: whether we feel comfortable or ill at ease, whether we feel a sense of belonging or alienation, whether we feel in control or at the mercy of others' private agendas. And the group in any meeting also has its own behaviour, governed by the principles of group dynamics. To ignore the behaviour of the group as a *group* is to risk mismanaging the meeting.

Secondly, the group is thinking together. This does not mean that we wish people to think *alike*. Far from it. We have gathered together because of our diverse views, experiences and expertise. We want people to voice different opinions; why else would we be asking them to attend? To be forced into thinking the same thoughts as a domineering Chair, or participant, is to waste the opportunity of the meeting. But we also need discipline in the meeting. Our conversation needs to be channelled. We should be thinking *together*: we should know the reason for meeting, the kind of thinking we should be engaged in at any point, and the desired outcome of the conversation. And we have a responsibility to help the group think together.

Why hold meetings?

The final part of our definition is that word 'purposefully'. Meetings are conversations with objectives. Yet too many meetings are held without clear objectives. In general, meetings are held with only four broad objectives:

- to discuss;
- to decide;
- to decree;
- to demolish.

Why do we hold meetings? The obvious answer is probably: 'To discuss things.' But *why* are we discussing them? And *how* should we discuss them? Unless we can answer these two questions clearly, the meeting will be in danger of degenerating into yet another 'talking shop', in which the group discusses to no purpose and achieves little.

Why discuss, then? 'To make decisions,' we might reply. But it's not clear that a meeting is always the best way to decide things. Making any decision is making a commitment to action, and gaining genuine commitment from a group can be difficult. Consensus – the usual word for collective decisions –

is often code for 'compromise'. Collective decisions are vulnerable to:

- analysis paralysis: spending too much time pondering unnecessary detail;
- the dead hand of the past: 'we've always done it this way';
- groupthink: the urge to agree for the sake of group unity, at the cost of considering alternatives.

Above all, it may not be necessary for the group to make the decision. Who will be taking action? And is the Chair perhaps using the meeting to gain support for a difficult or unpopular decision?

Decisions are best made by individuals. Action and accountability are clearer when one person takes responsibility for a decision. Of course, managers can call meetings to help them make better decisions: by generating ideas, different points of view, and support or sponsorship for their actions. However – at the risk of being controversial, for many, management meetings *are* called to decide things – we should challenge the principle of collective decision making itself.

We should also challenge the idea that meetings are an appropriate way to deliver information. Meetings are often called by senior management, who use a 'briefing' to announce their latest decrees, or by middle managers who are being 'put through their paces' in the familiar ritual of making a presentation to their seniors. Yet information presented in the context of a meeting will be largely forgotten unless it is supported in writing – particularly if the information is complex. And, if it's on paper, why hold the meeting?

What of 'demolishing'? Meetings are often called to play politics. And 'politics' usually means destructive behaviour of some sort. Of course, we can distinguish between influencing a meeting and wrecking it. The first is extremely common and may be acceptable. The second happens too often, though not always deliberately. Ignorance, clumsiness or lack of insight wreck more meetings than sabotage. Manipulating the meeting is another matter again. Manipulation is essentially covert. Its secret weapon is the 'hidden agenda'; its favoured strategy is to exploit the dynamics of group behaviour. Manipulators create alliances and sow the seeds of conflict; they confuse and divert and seek to outmanoeuvre the opposition. Meetings infected with manipulation tend to repeat themselves. The losers in one round will fight back in the next; reputations will be undermined and plans scuppered; cooperation gives way to stonewalling. Such situations can persist for years.

If we want to improve the quality of our meetings, we must start with a better sense of why we want to hold meetings at all. Here are some powerful reasons for holding meetings:

- *To exchange and evaluate information.* Meetings help us understand what others in the team are doing, and how it fits with our own work. Meetings help us to avoid duplicating tasks and locate our work in a larger context. In meetings, we can see the bigger picture.

  A group can evaluate information more effectively that a single person. In groups, we can bring multiple perspectives to bear on information, resulting in fewer gross errors of understanding. Gathering, exchanging and evaluating information are important activities in any organisation.

  Briefings exchange and evaluate information in a particular way. Staff survey consultations, or meetings between consultants and clients, all have this aim. Team leaders explain higher-level decisions and changes so that the team can see how they are affected. In exchange, the team can check their understanding, evaluate how the changes will affect their work and build their commitment to them. Critically, team briefings also allow the team to send their responses to change – and their own ideas – back 'up the line'.

- *To solve problems.* Virtually all meetings will involve problem solving of some kind. A group's success in solving a problem depends on the quality of its thinking: not how much thinking it does, but the *kind* of thinking it engages in. Problems need to be defined and the appropriate thinking tools chosen to tackle them. They tend to fit into two very broad categories: situations that are unsatisfactory in some way, or challenges arising from a change in circumstances.

  Groups are not good at solving problems that need expert knowledge or subtle reasoning. With such problems, the group will only think as well as its most competent member.
- *To resolve conflict.* Meetings can help to find the source of conflict and to explore different ways of dealing with it. The most obvious example of such a meeting would be a negotiation (though not all negotiations start from a position of conflict, of course).

  Conflict can easily arise within any kind of meeting. Solving problems and evaluating information can cause arguments that must be resolved if the group's thinking is to progress. Building or repairing morale at times of change and uncertainty can often mean resolving conflicts.
- *To inspire.* Humans are biologically gregarious. Very few of us can get through a day comfortably without interacting with others. We *like* to meet, especially in work situations that tend to isolate us from each other. Meetings give meaning to our work by relating it to the work of others; they can help us through difficulties by allowing us to share problems. The support of the group energises and motivates individuals to perform better. Group members who set their own goals often demand more of themselves than their superiors do.

David Hare, the playwright and screenwriter, has said that he is never bored in a theatre: excited and thrilled, or disappointed, frustrated and angry, but never indifferent. Meetings inspire similar feelings. Our responses to them are rarely neutral. We may emerge enthusiastic, committed and with a stronger sense of belonging, or exhausted by endless wrangling and barely suppressed feelings of violence.

Why meetings fail

Meetings are natural events. They appeal to deep-seated needs for social contact and a sense of belonging. For that reason alone, the damage done by poor meetings is probably far greater than we realise. A poorly managed meeting may cause more harm, in terms of frustration, confusion and poor morale, than a meeting that is cancelled.

There is usually no mystery about why meetings fail. We can identify a small number of factors that are at the heart of poor meetings management:

- *The meeting is unnecessary.* The job could be done in some simpler, cheaper way: it is routine and does not need to be discussed; information can be exchanged on paper or electronically. Perhaps only one or two people need to be involved, or the problem needs the attention of a single expert. Perhaps there is nothing to be done at all!
- *The meeting is held for the wrong reason.* To discuss, to decree or to demolish: all common reasons for holding meetings, and all inadequate. Managers often call meetings merely to wield power over others, or to pursue some private agenda. They use the meeting to rubberstamp or steamroller decisions.

  Many meetings happen as a matter of habit: a habit

that nobody dares challenge. They can be primarily social occasions, a chance to 'get away from the desk'. Meetings of this kind are group therapy in disguise: they are held to avoid loneliness.

- *The objective of the meeting is unclear.* Nobody has asked why the meeting is being held. Nobody knows its purpose, they have not received or read any of the supporting papers. The agenda is vague and unhelpful, or does not exist.
- *The wrong people are there.* Nobody present has the authority to make the required decisions. Perhaps the right people are absent: substitutes are sent at the last minute who are ill informed and unable to take responsibility.
- *Lack of proper control.* The procedure of the meeting is unclear; timekeeping is appalling; the discussion rambles from point to point; hidden agendas hijack the proceedings; conflict, when it occurs, is not properly managed. Blame for any or all of these problems is usually laid at the feet of a weak Chair, but a dictatorial Chair, who represses discussion rather than controlling it, can be just as damaging.
- *Poor environment.* The venue is inappropriate or uncomfortable; facilities are poor; disruptions destroy concentration.
- *Poor timing.* It is the wrong time of day/week/month/year to make the decision; the meeting fails to start or end on time; people arrive late or leave early.

Meetings will not improve by magic. They must be *managed.* You must want change – and be willing to implement it. You must also know the tools and techniques that will help you improve the quality of the meetings you attend – as a Chair, as a participant or as the administrator.

Improving the way a group of people thinks can be difficult. Sometimes only a policy decision will do the trick. Even if your organisation does not implement systematic change, you can change our own behaviour. If you hold – or attend – meetings, you have an opportunity to improve them. The longest journey starts with a single step, and somebody has to take it. Why not you?

The golden rules of effective meetings

This book is about how to manage meetings for everybody's benefit. Every idea and technique here is based on three golden rules:

1. *Every meeting is unique.* It has its own objectives. If there is no identifiable reason for holding the meeting, or if those objectives can be achieved in other ways, ask yourself whether the meeting is necessary.

   This is particularly so with regular meetings: weekly team meetings, project meetings or committee meetings. The agenda for every meeting must be unique. Meetings are too expensive to hold for no good reason.
2. *A meeting's success is judged by the actions that result from it.* Make a habit of writing an action list after every meeting you hold. What will happen after it finishes? Could you have agreed and delegated any of those actions without holding the meeting? Is responsibility for them allocated clearly to named individuals? Do they have exact deadlines? Who will monitor progress?

   If all we do at the end of a meeting is arrange another meeting, something has gone seriously wrong.
3. *Managing the meeting is everybody's responsibility.* Obviously, the Chair bears the primary responsibility

for how the meeting is conducted. But each participant has a role to play. The administrator or minute-taker, too, can play a major role in managing the meeting: keeping time, summarising, collating action points and, of course, completing an accurate record of the meeting's progress and outcomes.

2

How groups work

A meeting is a group in action. To manage meetings more effectively, we need to know something about how groups behave. The group may be completely new, or meeting only once; it may be a newly formed team or a regular committee. Knowing how people behave in groups will allow us to:

- understand better what is actually going on in a meeting;
- appreciate why conversations in groups differ from conversations between individuals;
- anticipate conflict and prevent or tackle it;
- manage the group's behaviour;
- improve the output or results of the meeting.

So we must examine how groups develop, the structures within groups that emerge from that process and how those structures encourage or discourage certain kinds of behaviour in our meetings.

We can define a group as any number of people who:

- interact with each other in some way;
- are aware of each other;
- perceive themselves to be a group.

This distinguishes groups from crowds or collections of individuals. A viable group, by our definition, is limited in numbers to about 12: any meeting involving more will have difficulty in thinking as a group, and subgroups will emerge. Annual General Meetings and other big meetings need rigorous procedures to overcome this tendency inherent in large numbers of people to splinter or collapse into a crowd.

Groups can be formal or informal. Formal groups are consciously created by organisations to accomplish particular tasks or fulfil specific functions. Teams are formal groups. They may be permanent or temporary: administrative teams or project teams, for example. Informal teams emerge spontaneously from the interaction of individuals as they associate with each other, talking, joking, exchanging experiences and generally enjoying each other's company. Both kinds of group exist in organisations. Informal groups, broadly speaking, satisfy the human needs that formal groups neglect or ignore. The more formal the group, the more task-oriented it will be; the more informal, the more socially-oriented.

Groups have two kinds of objectives: task objectives and social objectives. *Task objectives* define the group's work and may be imposed or dictated from outside the group. *Social objectives* concern the group's developing sense of identity, its well-being and the relationships of group members to each other and to the group. They usually develop from within the group.

A group in a meeting will pursue *both* kinds of objectives. Problems can arise when task and social objectives become mismatched. For example, task objectives may become obscured by social objectives (the group is having too much of a good time). Task objectives may suppress or damage social objectives (tasks imposed dictatorially, for example, or when the group is under stress). The two kinds of objective may even come into conflict (for example, one part of the group seeking to impose tasks on another).

It is generally agreed that, the more cohesive a group, the

more productive it is. A group's cohesion emerges from mutually positive attitudes among group members, and is expressed in terms of both task and social objectives. If both task and social objectives are weak, the group's cohesion will be poor and its performance will certainly suffer. Many meetings flounder because neither the objectives nor the group's sense of identity are clear; the conversation becomes confused and sometimes hostile.

Strong task objectives and poor social objectives may be somewhat effective: a meeting can get things done in a 'bad atmosphere', though at the cost of anxiety, stress, antagonism, frustration and hurt feelings. Achieving task objectives, of course, can strengthen social cohesion. Strong social objectives without a clear focus on task objectives can be just as damaging. A meeting where everybody is only 'bonding' or basking in self-congratulation will not be highly productive.

Both task and social objectives must be managed if we want to improve our meetings. Clarifying task objectives is fundamental: identifying our goals, expressing them clearly on an agenda, keeping the meeting focused on results. But we ignore social objectives at our peril. Our ability to manage and influence the relationships within the group is as important as our ability to keep the meeting's collective eye 'on the ball'.

Individuals and groups

A group is made up of individuals. Once introduced into a group, our primary aim is to integrate. As individuals, we pursue the essential aims of:

- well-being (physical, mental, emotional, economic, spiritual);
- a sense of belonging;
- recognition from the group;
- control over our own lives.

If the group satisfies these needs, we will respond by strengthening it. If we doubt that the group will satisfy them, we may not participate fully. If we become convinced that the group can't or won't support us, we will withdraw – physically or mentally – or pursue some other strategy. We may seek to create a subgroup, or threaten the group's identity by engaging in sabotage.

The group itself, meanwhile, begins to take on a life of its own. Its primary objective is to survive. If counteracting forces become too strong and the group splinters, new groups will start to form at once.

Groups affect individuals' behaviour; in turn, we can influence the groups we join. It is the complicated web of relationships within the group that is important.

How groups develop

Groups are alive. They develop continually. A group may form, grow and destroy itself in a matter of hours; another may be stuck at one stage for months or even years. Barry Tuckman's (1965) four-stage model of a group's evolution, from inception to full maturity, has proved highly influential.

1. Forming

At the first stage, individuals have not yet become a group. Relationships are tentative. We are finding out about each other: our attitudes, background and values. We are also keen to establish our own identities and make an impression. It is a time of some anxiety and potential embarrassment. In a meeting, the Chair must strengthen the group quickly, by identifying what binds it together and by stating the rules governing its behaviour.

2. Storming

This second stage is characterised by conflict. Group members challenge each other's versions of reality. Value systems (what we regard as important) and belief systems (the truths we hold to be self-evident) are thrashed out. At a dinner party, this conflict is the 'politics and religion' stage, and can be uncomfortable; in a meeting, versions of reality may be disguised in terms of action: preferred methods of working.

Relationships established in the forming stage might be disrupted or destroyed. Individuals will try tactical manoeuvres: seeking allies, withdrawing ('wait and see'), empire building, vetoing, threatening to disrupt the proceedings, demanding the right to be recognised, resisting an onslaught against them. The group will try to resolve this conflict by agreeing a version of reality: the value and belief systems to which everybody can 'sign up'.

3. Norming

The group has found a shared frame of reference: an agreed version of reality based on common perceptions, values and beliefs. These are the group's norms. It now develops a way of working to achieve its goals, allocating roles and rules of conduct: a practical framework in which people can work together. It is at this stage that groupthink can emerge. Anybody who refuses to accept the norms may be labelled as 'deviant' or 'subversive'. The group will apply increasingly painful pressure on them to conform.

4. Performing

The group gets on with the job in hand. It is fully mature.

Not all groups develop this far. Many groups become stuck in an early stage – sometimes irretrievably. Others bounce back and forth between stages, or revert to an earlier stage with a change of membership.

Tuckman's model can help us in two ways. We can use it to help improve the performance of our meetings, and it can indicate why a particular meeting may be going wrong. A group cannot evolve healthily from one stage to the next if issues in the earlier stage remain unresolved. Group leaders may try to reach the performing stage without having agreed a frame of reference in the norming stage. A meeting may suffer at the norming stage because common values and goals have been left unclear. Participants may continue to manipulate the group to achieve personal, 'political' goals, dragging it back into storming, or even destroying it completely so that forming must start anew.

Understanding the structure of groups

As the group evolves through these four stages, it develops a structure. We seek predictability in a group: uncertainty about others' behaviour is threatening. The group's structure provides a 'system of solutions' to this threat of unpredictable behaviour.

Group structure is neither fixed nor permanent. It is a complex, dynamic system, operating along a number of dimensions, including:

- status;
- power;
- role;
- leadership;
- liking.

We can interpret people's behaviour in a meeting as evidence of their efforts to find their place in the group structure, to move within it or to challenge it.

Status

Each position in the group has a value assigned to it. This status may arise formally or socially. Formal status is the collection of rights and duties associated with a position. Social status is the rank of a person as measured by the group: the degree of respect, familiarity or reserve the group gives to that person.

Our status in a group is always at risk. A group confers status on anybody who meets the group's expectations. Our status is created entirely through others' perceptions (we may call it 'good name' or 'reputation'). It can be destroyed or diminished in a moment. Downgrading a person's status in the group can be a powerful way of exerting the group's authority.

Power

Power is the control we can exert over others. If we can influence or control people's behaviour in any way, we have power over them. John French and Bertram Raven (1959) identified five kinds of power:

1. *reward power:* the ability to grant favours for behaviour;
2. *coercive power:* the ability to punish others;
3. *legitimate power:* conferred by law or other sets of rules;
4. *referent power:* the 'charisma' that causes others to imitate or idolise;
5. *expert power:* deriving from specific levels of knowledge or skill.

People may seek to exercise different kinds of power at different times. A participant in a meeting with little reward power may seize an opportunity to influence the meeting as an expert; a Chair lacking charisma or respect may try to exert authority by appealing to legitimate or even coercive power.

A group can exercise power of its own. Norms – the accepted rules of engagement within the group, and the agreed view of reality that members of the group share – are the means by which the group wields power. To resist or violate group norms threatens the very identity of the group. Groups will, therefore, often pressurise people to conform. Group members may be:

- *encouraged:* by humour, gentle sarcasm, pointed remarks;
- *embarrassed:* categorised as weak, stupid, irresponsible, odd – even evil;
- *excluded:* temporarily but deliberately left out of the conversation; or
- *expelled:* told to 'shut up or get out'.

The pressure to conform to group norms can be enormous. We may feel inhibited from voicing opinions or ideas; we may even find ourselves uttering or agreeing to ideas that we would not support outside the group. We may even see the world differently once we have joined a group.

As participants, we can respond to this pressure in one of three ways. We can:

- argue our case, fight our corner and try to persuade others to join us;
- conform and suppress any opinion or behaviour that offends the group;
- withdraw ('There is a world elsewhere', to quote Shakespeare's *Coriolanus*).

What we do will depend on our location in the group structure. If we have a great deal of power, we may easily persuade the group to change its norms in our favour. If we have high status or are much liked, the group may tolerate deviant behaviour rather than lose a valuable member.

Role

Our role in the meeting is the set of behaviours expected of us by the group. Charles Handy (1976) has suggested that, when we join a group, we ask three questions:

1. *What is my identity in the group?* What is my task role? What do people expect me to do?
2. *Where is power located in the group?* Who has it? What kind is it? Do I want to exert power of any kind?
3. *What are my objectives?* What do I need? Are they in line with those of the group? What will I do if they are not?

Our answers to these questions will guide us towards the roles we play in the group.

Task roles have been explored extensively. Meredith Belbin's are probably the most famous. Thousands of managers have now used Belbin's (1981) questionnaire to locate themselves among his categories of:

- chair/coordinator;
- shaper/team leader;
- plant/innovator or creative thinker;
- monitor-evaluator/critical thinker;
- company worker/implementer;
- team worker/team builder;
- finisher/detail checker and pusher;
- resource investigator/researcher outside the team.

Recently, Belbin has felt the need to add a further role, that of 'expert'. A successful team will contain a balance of all nine roles; a team too strong in any one or more will perform less successfully. The same may be said of meetings, though our ability to improve the balance by changing the group may be limited.

Social roles have been investigated in numerous ways. We may recognise a few traditional social roles in meetings: the mediator, the devil's advocate, and the licensed fool. A well-established technique distinguishes between aggressive, passive and assertive behaviour. This simple model serves to identify different social roles in a group in terms of the way we exercise our strength with others. Other models are more complex. Transactional Analysis, for example, identifies relationships between 'parents', 'children' and 'adults' and suggests how we can improve our social transactions with others by recognising which roles we use in specific situations.

Leadership

This dimension of group structure is closely related to all the others, even if a leader is imposed on the group from outside.

We can define leadership as behaviour that helps the group to achieve its preferred objectives. Research in the 1950s distinguished between autocratic, democratic and *laissez-faire* styles of leadership and their respective effects on the performance of groups. The concept of leadership itself has changed radically since then, as command-and-control structures in organisations have given way – at least to some extent – to matrix structures. Leadership is now often referred to as a 'facilitative' activity: doing whatever *allows* the group to achieve, rather than directing people's energy in a certain direction.

It is useful, particularly in the context of meetings, to distinguish between task leadership and process leadership. The first focuses on the job to be done, the second on building good relations within the group.

Liking

The liking dimension emerges spontaneously, helping to gain people status or power, or allowing them to exercise effective leadership.

The simple distinction between liking and disliking seems crude. We can find others attractive in many different ways or take against them in ways we may not be able – or willing – to articulate. Liking can become an emotional entanglement or even a fully-fledged relationship; dislike can turn into a vendetta or a curious, half-coded game of tit-for-tat. We may be unaware of the structures of like and dislike in the group at a meeting, and may have to rely on clues.

How groups behave

Broadly, we can define behaviour in meetings as *task behaviour* (contributions to the meeting's work) and *process behaviour* (helping the group to develop).

A third category, *non-functional behaviour*, includes anything that hinders or prevents the meetings from succeeding in either its task or process objectives. Distinguishing between these three categories can be difficult, especially if the meeting includes people of different cultural backgrounds. As the Chair of a meeting, focusing on objectives and targets – as well as the clock – you will be hard pressed to identify more than a few of these behaviours. You may be reacting to many of them unconsciously.

Separating task direction from process direction can be useful. Using video or, better still, an external meetings auditor, is valuable. Picking and responding to only a few of these behaviours, then encouraging or discouraging them, can improve the group's performance substantially.

Group behaviours

Task behaviours

- initiating: defining a problem, redefining it, making suggestions, presenting new information, proposing solutions
- seeking information
- giving information
- setting standards
- coordinating: relating ideas to each other, comparing information
- building and elaborating: developing ideas, giving examples, adding detail, creating scenarios
- summarising: restating, reorganising information, repeating, clarifying
- evaluating: for value or relevance
- diagnosing: seeking causes of problems
- testing for consensus or disagreement

Process behaviours

- encouraging: responding positively, praising, accepting
- gate-keeping: letting others contribute
- stopping: ending a line of argument that seems unproductive or counter-intuitive
- following: listening and triggering more from others
- redirecting: from one person to another
- expressing group feeling
- mediating: in moments of conflict
- relieving tension: by suggesting a break or injecting humour

Non-functional behaviours

- aggression
- blocking
- self-confessing or sympathy seeking
- competing
- special pleading
- seeking attention
- negative or offensive humour
- withdrawing

Managing the group

How then, can we manage a group? It all seems so complicated! Managing people as individuals can be hard enough; managing groups of people looks well nigh impossible. Group dynamics and group development; the webs of status and power within the group; the fleeting and complicated behaviours that groups exhibit as they try to work together – where can we start?

The first lesson is perhaps the hardest. If we don't manage the group, the group will manage itself. The key – for the Chair, and for any participant who wants to fulfil his or her responsibility and contribute positively to a meeting – is to understand this simple fact and work *with* the group rather than *against* it. Here are some simple questions to set you thinking:

- *Can you see the group in this meeting as a group?* Or are they individuals who have little relationship to each other?
- *Are there obvious subgroups within the group?* When a client group meets a supplier or provider group, for example, links within the subgroups will be stronger than between the two groups – at least to start with. The same will be true of meetings between management and unions, or between different departments in a large organisation.
- *Can you clearly identify task and social objectives for the group?* Both need to be clear. Announce task objectives at the start of the meeting. It might also be worth building in a short 'social' period, in which people can get to know each other, swap gossip or 'network'. The group's ability to think and work well depends as much on the relationships within the group as on clear task definition.
- *Can you identify any individual needs that may interfere with the objectives of the meeting?* Most 'people

issues' in meetings can be traced back to an individual need that the group is not fulfilling, for some reason. Some such issues can become chronic problems. Can you at least be forewarned of these issues? Perhaps you can take action to address that need within the meeting itself.

- *How far has the group developed?* Where is it in the Tuckman cycle? There are specific actions a Chair can take to guide a group through each stage. Perhaps the group will move through one or more stages during the meeting itself:
  - At the *forming* stage, establish the purpose of the meeting, and the rules of engagement. Introduce everybody and allow them to state their relationship to the group and to the agenda.
  - At the *storming* stage – probably the most difficult stage for any group – the Chair needs to do everything possible to discourage argument, not by quashing it but by encouraging diverse ideas. Work through different points of view towards an agreed view of the situation: what the problem is, what our objective is, how we agree to behave.
  - At the *norming* stage, beware the 'feel-good factor'. Groupthink can be just as damaging to the meeting's outcome as conflict. Judgement can falter; dissidents may be sidelined. Concentrate on opportunities for action and on planning. Seek to include any participants who seem left out. Challenge majority opinions.
  - If you are lucky enough to be working with a group that has reached the *performing* stage, you should be able to exercise minimal control and allow the group to do the work itself. Concentrate on requests for action. Allocate tasks. Set deadlines.

- *How can you influence the group's structure?* You may be able to identify where status or power are influential in the group. You may see people with high status or power as a threat to the group's well-being – or to your own authority as Chair. Perhaps you want to weaken such influences, or undermine them. It might be better to work with these influences by channelling them towards the task objectives of the meeting. Give a powerful individual a challenging task; use status to build a team of co-workers within a project.

  Managing roles in the group can be even more difficult – especially if you subscribe to Belbin's fairly complicated system of team roles. Once you are able to identify people's role-playing abilities and preferences, you may be able to use those abilities to the group's advantage. Exploit the creativity of your 'plants' and the thoroughness of the 'shapers' and 'finishers'. Use the diplomatic skills of the 'team workers' to weld the group together.
- *What behaviours do you want to encourage in the group?* Think of the range of task and process behaviours in the group as a repertoire of behaviours that you can encourage and 'play', through your management of the conversation. Challenge non-functional behaviours rather than letting them take control. This is undoubtedly the most complicated aspect of leading a meeting; acquiring the skills of behaviour management is not achieved overnight.

Group dynamics are complicated. It's little wonder that many of us find it difficult to manage a group of people in a meeting. Let's recap all the main ideas we've explored in this chapter.

Summary

A meeting is a group in action. Groups can be formal or informal. Groups have two kinds of objectives: task objectives and social objectives. A group in a meeting will pursue both kinds of objectives. It is generally agreed that, the more cohesive a group, the more productive it is. Both task and social objectives must be managed if we want to improve our meetings.

A group is made up of individuals. Once introduced into a group, our primary aim is to integrate. If we become convinced that the group can't or won't support us, we will withdraw – physically or mentally. The group itself, meanwhile, begins to take on a life of its own.

Groups affect individuals' behaviour; in turn, we can influence the groups we join.

Groups are alive. They develop continually. We can identify four stages in the history of group development:

1. *Forming.* At the first stage, individuals have not yet become a group.
2. *Storming.* The second stage is characterised by conflict.
3. *Norming.* At the third stage, the group has found a shared frame of reference and a set of norms.
4. *Performing.* At the fourth stage, the group gets on with the job in hand. It is fully mature.

This four-stage model can help us manage meetings in two ways: we can use it to help our meetings improve their performance, and the model can indicate why a particular meeting may be going wrong.

As the group evolves through these four stages, it develops a structure. Group structure is a complex, dynamic system, operating along a number of dimensions, including:

- status;
- power;
- role;
- leadership;
- liking.

Each position in the group has a value assigned to it. Our status in a group is always at risk.

Power is the control we can exert over others. We can identify five kinds of power:

1. *reward power:* the ability to grant favours for behaviour;
2. *coercive power:* the ability to punish others;
3. *legitimate power:* conferred by law or other sets of rules;
4. *referent power:* the 'charisma' that causes others to imitate or idolise;
5. *expert power:* deriving from knowledge or skill.

People may seek to exercise different kinds of power at different times. A group can exercise power of its own, through the norms that it creates for itself.

Groups often pressurise people to conform. Group members may be:

- *encouraged:* by humour, gentle sarcasm, pointed remarks;
- *embarrassed:* categorised as weak, stupid, irresponsible, odd – even evil;
- *excluded:* temporarily but deliberately left out of the conversation; or
- *expelled:* told to 'shut up or get out'.

The pressure to conform to group norms can be enormous. As participants, we can respond to this pressure in one of three ways. We can argue our case, fight our corner and try to persuade others to join us; or we can conform and suppress any opinion or behaviour that offends the group; or we can withdraw.

Our role in the meeting is the set of behaviours expected of us by the group. Task roles and social roles have been investigated in numerous ways.

We can define leadership as behaviour that helps the group to achieve its preferred objectives. It is useful, particularly in the context of meetings, to distinguish between task leadership and process leadership.

The liking dimension emerges spontaneously. We may be unaware of the structures of like and dislike in the group at a meeting, and may have to rely on clues.

Broadly, we can define behaviour in meetings as task behaviour: contributions to the meeting's work; process behaviour: helping the group to develop; and non-functional behaviour. In managing the group's behaviour, it can be useful to separate task direction from process direction.

If we don't manage the group, the group will manage itself. The key – for the Chair, and for any participant who wants to fulfil his or her responsibility and contribute positively to a meeting – is to understand this simple fact and work *with* the group rather than *against* it.

Every chapter in this book deals in more depth with themes that we've touched on here. Meanwhile, here is a checklist of practical suggestions that will put you on the right track:

- Make task objectives clear.
- Thank people for their contributions.
- Encourage different points of view.
- Challenge opinions or statements for relevance and ask for evidence.
- Encourage people to cooperate.
- Challenge behaviour that threatens or subverts the group: political remarks, evidence of hidden agendas, personal attacks.

- Give people clear task responsibilities.
- Remind the group often of the meeting's objective.
- Move things forward.
- Emphasise achievement in the meeting.
- Limit chat and gossip.

3

Preparing for the meeting

Ninety per cent of an effective meeting happens before it takes place. Even the briefest or most informal meeting benefits from preparation, even if it is only a few notes scribbled on the back of an envelope. A more formal meeting, involving more than a very few people, must be organised thoroughly.

Clarifying your objectives

Establish the purpose of the meeting. Don't trust to imagination or memory. Write it down: this will form the basis of the meeting's title:

> I am calling this meeting to...

Your statement of purpose should revolve around a verb. What are you going to *do* – apart from talk? If you are going to address a number of tasks, they should be connected in some way. Are they all relevant to all the members of the group? Is the meeting necessary to carry them all out? Some tasks might be dealt with more efficiently in 'mini-meetings' before or after the main meeting, without wasting the whole group's time.

What do you want to achieve? Perhaps you will need to consider:

- the ideal outcome;
- the realistic outcome;
- a fallback position.

What decisions need to be taken in the meeting? Who will take them? Why must the decision be made *at the meeting*? Are resources available to carry out any actions that you anticipate emerging from the meeting? Is anybody else going to be affected? Should you perhaps consult those people – or even invite them to the meeting?

Who is involved?

Well: you are, for a start! What is *your* role in this meeting? Are you taking the role of leader, Chair, facilitator or whatever term suits you? Is there a good reason for you to take command? Or is it merely force of habit that puts you in this position? You could consider rotating the role of Chair in the meeting, or from meeting to meeting, so that everybody in the team has the opportunity to take and experience that tricky responsibility. At the very least, people may become less willing to 'misbehave' when they know that it's their turn to keep order next time!

Who is participating?

Think about the other people who will be attending. Are they the right people? What is their relevance to the meeting's purpose? Are there any particular kinds of contribution you want them to make, or that they intend to make? Perhaps they are:

- key decision makers;
- experts or givers of information;
- people who need information;
- opinion formers;
- senior managers with an interest in the decisions to be reached;
- arbitrators in potential disputes;
- friends, consultants or guests.

Are they able to attend? The more valuable they are to the meeting, the less likely they are to be available! Will a deputy or last minute substitute be acceptable? What do they need to prepare for the meeting? Should you brief them or send them papers: the minutes of the last meeting, reports, the latest figures?

Look over your agenda and try to allocate names to items. Who is responsible for the task under discussion? Who will need to take the critical decision? Who will carry it through? Consider putting them in charge of the task, allowing you to oversee the conversation.

What roles do you expect people to play? We have already seen that the roles people adopt in meetings contribute to the way a group structures itself and behaves. A role is a set of behaviours by which we can help the meeting achieve its objectives. Most of us tend to contribute to groups in consistent ways. We can broadly categorise these types as:

- ideas people;
- action people;
- administrators;
- carers.

The typical behaviours and characteristics of each type are shown in the box below. Ideally, the group should contain a balance of all four. To adjust the balance in the group, you may need to ask somebody to play a certain role more strongly than normal.

Roles in meetings

Ideas people

Typical behaviours
Advancing new ideas and strategies
Focusing on major issues
Tackling problem solving creatively
Exploring and reporting on ideas and developments beyond the meeting
Making contacts outside the group

Positive qualities
Imagination, intellect, knowledge
Willing to explore
Can make contact with others

Possible weaknesses
May disregard practical details, rules or regulations
Short attention span

Action people

Typical behaviours
Influencing the way the meeting's thinking is channelled

Administrators

Typical behaviours
Analysing problems, evaluating ideas and suggestions for practicability
Ensuring nothing has been overlooked
Checking details
Carrying out agreed plans systematically and efficiently

Positive qualities
Organisational ability, practicality, common sense of judgement, discretion

Possible weaknesses
May lack inspiration
Inability to motivate others
Tendency to worry about details
Reluctant to let go

Carers

Typical behaviours
Co-ordinating the meeting's progress
Making best use of the group's resources

(Action people continued)
Focusing on objectives and priorities
Pushing towards a decision
Turning concepts and plans into practical working procedures
Maintaining a sense of urgency

Positive qualities
Drive and a readiness to challenge inertia, ineffectiveness, complacency and self-deception
Capacity to follow through
Self-discipline

Possible weaknesses
Prone to provocation, irritation and impatience
Lack of flexibility
May be unresponsive to new or unproven ideas

(Carers continued)
Maximising the potential of each team member
Building on suggestions
Improving communication within the group

Positive qualities
Welcomes all contributions on their merit
Strong sense of objectives
Ability to respond to people and situations
Promotes team spirit

Possible weaknesses
May try to avoid conflict
May be indecisive in moments of crisis

Many meetings fail because the group is dominated by one or two roles. This situation often arises in teams made up of professional or technical specialists promoted to managerial positions. A group of ideas people may be enormously creative but may never get anything done. A group of action people may spend all their time arguing about what to do, pitching one solution against another without investigating causes or different perspectives on the problem. A group of administrators may pay great attention to 'the dots and commas' but fail to come up with new solutions. A group of carers may look after each other but fail to address difficult or contentious issues.

Do the participants form a natural group? How well do they know each other? What are their interests, aims, ambitions and assumptions about each other? Do you envisage conflicts between any of these interests and ambitions? Where is the common ground between them?

How many people will attend? Meetings often go out of control simply because too many people are present. There is a famous saying: 'The usefulness of a meeting is in inverse proportion to the number of people attending.' The ideal number for an internal business meeting is between six and nine. Why?

- A group of this size has a high productivity rate.
- Individuals are less likely to be swallowed up in a crowd.
- Cliques are less likely to form.
- The group is easier to control.

How many is enough?

Size of group	Advantages	Disadvantages
Small group (2–5)	Cohesive High productivity All participants visible Low absenteeism likely Less danger of cliques	Narrow range of skills Hard to generate conversation Poor evaluation of information
Large group (10+)	Better evaluation of information Group pressure on saboteurs	Hard to get agreement Need for more control People scared into silence High absenteeism Meetings within the meeting Danger of cliques

What do the participants need to prepare for the meeting? Should you brief them, or send them papers: the minutes of the last meeting, reports, the latest figures?

Three key roles

So far, we can see two clear roles emerging in the management of meetings. The Chair manages the *process* of the meeting; the participants have task responsibilities and manage the *content* of the meeting.

Many Chairs feel that they have the responsibility – and the right – to 'steer' the meeting, directing the conversation towards the results they themselves want. 'Steering' the meeting is popular with some captains of industry, who have learnt how to run meetings only from watching their predecessors and who regard manipulating outcomes in meetings as part of the job description. Such a dictatorial approach may also be the result of habit; it may simply result from ignorance.

There is a subtle distinction to be made here. Of course a meeting must be planned and the conversation guided towards desired outcomes. But controlling the *process* of the conversation is not the same as controlling the *task*. Process management is the complex job of listening to and guiding the conversation. Think of it as 'air traffic control'. Task control is like flying an aircraft to its destination: defining the task, managing information, solving problems and making decisions.

Mix process management with task management, and the meeting is likely to fail. Many managers still try to manage business meetings without understanding this critical distinction. The solution is to separate these two roles and allocate them to different people. The Chair – managing the process of the conversation – becomes an 'air traffic controller'. He or she controls group communication, guiding, disciplining and redirecting as necessary. The Chair is indeed 'steering' the conversation, but like the pilot on a ship, negotiating the reefs and channels of the conversation.

Some participants become 'task owners', responsible for defining the task and achieving it. They are like the ship's captain, with a clear destination in mind and in command of the overall course of the conversation. Consider delegating task ownership to the group member whose job or work is most closely affected by the item under discussion. He or she is best placed to specify what to discuss, what information is needed, what he or she expects the group to contribute and what kind of outcome he or she is seeking. Other participants can then act as 'thinking resources', contributing ideas and analysis as required.

A third essential role is that of recorder or minute-taker. I prefer the term 'meeting administrator': it more accurately defines the range of responsibilities this person usually takes on. At the heart of his or her responsibilities is taking an accurate record of the meeting: what happens, what is discussed, what is decided and what actions are agreed. But the administrator can also take on other responsibilities relating to managing the meeting's process.

These three roles are at the heart of managing meetings. Although real life often forces one person to share two – or even all – of these roles, in the best meetings they are split and are taken by different people.

Effective meetings: three key roles

Chair	***Process director***	Controls communications traffic Manages time Manages social objectives Oversees group development Specifies meeting structure Controls conversation

		Specifies how the group is to think Summarises and reflects the group's thinking
Participant	***Task owner***	Sets objective of thinking process Presents relevant information States when task is achieved Measures success of outcomes
	Thinking resource	Contributes ideas or information Helps in thinking and solving problems A 'consultant' to the task owner
Administrator	***Recorder***	Records meeting Can help with time management Can help to maintain order in the interests of a clear record Can summarise at the end of agenda items and at the end of the meeting

When and where?

Any meeting can be affected by when and where it's held. Of course, many meetings arrange their own times and venues. The decision must be made today and not next week; the conference room is only available at 2 o'clock; and so on. Within the inevitable constraints of a busy organisation, do what you can to influence these matters for the better.

Times and timings

Is the date of the meeting auspicious? Can everybody attend? Is it close enough to register in people's memories, and far enough ahead to allow them to prepare? Is it a 'good' day of the week?

We are all more alert at certain times of the day than at

others. Research suggests that the best time for thinking is late morning: a finding confirmed by the international air company which made it policy a few years ago for all meetings to be held in one of two slots: 9–11 am and 11 am–1 pm. Meeting at the end of the day might spur people to make their meetings shorter, but it might not make them better. Consider, also, other ways to save time. It may be possible, for example, to arrange the meeting in conjunction with others to make the best use of people's time.

Are your meetings too long? It is a recurrent complaint. Some Chairs seem to make it a point of honour to have meetings that last for hours. But longer does not mean better. A successful meeting depends on how much – and how well – everybody participates, not on how long it is.

Incredibly, many meetings still begin without any agreed finishing time. 'We just go on until we've finished', sighs the beleaguered Chair. This is a major problem. Nothing does more harm to concentration and discipline than an open-ended meeting. The agenda should announce a finishing time; and the Chair should keep to it.

The meeting's venue

The venue can be as critical to a meeting's success as the time of day it's held. Is the venue conveniently located? Is it accessible: for people with disabilities, for example, or women travelling alone at night? Are you meeting on 'home ground'? Will everybody feel at ease when they are in the room? I remember one meeting where most of us felt distinctly intimidated by the trophies of a dominant senior manager, hung around the walls. If the meeting is in a hotel or conference venue, you will need to liaise with hotel staff to establish timings, numbers, catering and needs for equipment.

Is the room the right size and shape? Is it suitable for your purpose? Consider:

- acoustics;
- heating, lighting and ventilation;
- chairs: quantity and comfort;
- tables: size, flexibility and sturdiness;
- equipment and power points;
- procedures: fire drill, refreshments, toilets, telephones;
- distractions: air-conditioning, trains, noise, the view, building work, intercoms.

You must also consider the furniture and how it is laid out, both in terms of group dynamics, and in relation to doors and windows. What can you move? Are the furniture and fittings:

- *fixed:* walls, windows, doors;
- *semi-fixed:* partitions, seating, projection screens. whiteboards;
- *movable:* chairs, tables, equipment.

Be careful not to regard semi-fixed fittings as fixed! You may lose an opportunity to adapt a room better to your needs.

The layout of furniture you choose will depend on the style of meeting you want to adopt. The Chair may wish to place allies (or potential troublemakers!) in 'control positions'. The administrator should be able to communicate easily with everybody – and especially the Chair – while taking the minutes. Everybody should be able to see a screen or flipchart with a minimum of disruption.

Effective participation depends on easy eye contact. Participants should be about one arm's length from each other. Closer, and they will invade each other's space; further apart, they will feel isolated and the group dynamics will suffer.

Setting the procedure

Give careful thought to how you will conduct the meeting. The Chair's task is to release the talents of the group assembled round the table. How do you intend to make the most of the skills and experience at your disposal?

Your procedural style will determine how the meeting – well, proceeds! What type of meeting is it? Do you have to abide by regulations or legal requirements in the way you run the meeting? How do you expect participants to contribute? How will you control the conversation? Will everybody address their remarks, formally, through the Chair? Or perhaps you will opt for a policy of minimal control: doing no more than announcing each item, summarising discussion, calling for a formal decision – and, crucially, keeping to time.

Preparing briefing papers

Briefing papers often form the basis for conversations in meetings. These may outline the issue to be discussed in some detail, give background information and indicate the preferred direction the 'task owner' would like the meeting to take. They may also form the basis of a formal presentation at the meeting.

The main risk, of course, is that the papers may not be read. The more papers the participants face, the less likely they are to read all of them. You are probably battling for your reader's attention. You must make your paper as readable as possible and put points over as explicitly as you can.

Knowing what points to make can itself be difficult. You may not be clear what is expected of you, or what you can suggest without overstepping your authority. As a result, many briefing papers are indigestible. Using the traditional report structure – introduction, findings, conclusion, recommendations – may not help. In fact, it often results in one of two kinds of briefing paper, which should be avoided at all costs!

The first is *the storyline*. This is the paper that begins at the very beginning and labours heavily towards its conclusion. Writers usually justify writing storylines by asserting that the meeting 'must know all the background in order to understand the conclusion'. In fact, readers are unlikely to bother with a narrative when they cannot see its relevance.

The second is *the stream of consciousness*. Here, the writer puts down thoughts in exactly the order in which they occurred. Writers will justify the stream of consciousness by saying: 'I want the reader to follow the course of my thinking.' Unfortunately, if the readers can see no *reason* to follow your reasoning, they probably will not bother to follow.

The critical point is that your paper must contain *only* the information necessary to support your ideas – not everything you know about the topic. An effective briefing paper is well planned. Planning the paper, like planning anything else, is a *design* process. And the design that delivers information most clearly to most readers is a pyramid.

A pyramid structure organises your ideas into a hierarchy. At the top of the pyramid is a message. This is your governing idea: the thought that you want the readers to grasp, even if they fail to read another word. The message is then supported by a small number of key points – also ideas – that explain or fill out the message in more detail. These points are then in turn supported by information that fills out your ideas still further.

Here's how to build your pyramid structure:

- *Establish the purpose of the paper.* What are you trying to achieve in this paper? Most business documents seek either to persuade or explain. Briefing papers are no different. In particular, are you recommending, or offering options (two of the most common purposes of such papers)?
- *Think about your audience.* How will the committee, board or meeting act in response to your paper? What information do they need? What do they already

know? What more do they need to know? What do they value or find important? What will convince them?

- *Work out your key message.* You should be able to express your governing idea in a simple sentence of no more than about 15 words. Place it, prominently, at the beginning of the paper, as the summary. Make sure that your message clearly expresses your purpose.
- *Work out the key points you need to make to support the message.* Each key point can form the core of a section of the paper, if necessary. Keep the number of key points small in number: no more than six, no matter how big or complicated the subject may be.
- *Throughout the paper, remember to make points and support them.* Do not give more information than is necessary to support your points; resist going into detail as much as you can. Make your style assertive and proactive.

Working with the administrator

The administrator of the meeting is usually more than a minute-taker, important though that function is. The administrator will often have responsibility for much of the preparation for the meeting, arrangements during the meeting and follow-up after it.

The main complaints voiced by meeting administrators are that they:

- have been brought in at a moment's notice;
- are unclear what their responsibilities are;
- have not been told what style to adopt in writing minutes;
- do not understand what people are talking about;

- do not know participants or their names;
- are overwhelmed by jargon;
- cannot follow a conversation because it is disorderly;
- get bored during the meeting through lack of involvement;
- are unclear what has been agreed or resolved;
- have their minutes 'doctored' or 'censored' by the Chair (or others).

The Chair can forestall many of these common problems. He or she should involve the administrator in – or at the very least inform them of – all the preparations. A 'pre-meeting meeting' can be useful. At this meeting, Chair and administrator can agree:

- the purpose of the meeting;
- who is attending;
- what will go on the agenda;
- background information to help in taking the minutes.

How will you record the meeting's progress? Do not be hidebound by tradition: consider how to improve the minutes of the meeting. The administrator will be able to take the minutes more effectively if he or she has the authority to intervene to clarify points that are unclear and summarise at the end of each item with details of decisions and actions agreed.

Talk together about these matters *before the meeting*. The administrator can be invaluable in helping the Chair during the meeting to keep time, to keep to the agenda and to keep order. Taking on these responsibilities will make administering the meeting itself more satisfying.

4

What's on the agenda?

Every meeting has an agenda. Many have more than one agenda running at the same time! The agenda may not have been written down, discussed or even thought about. But the agenda is there, all the same. And whoever controls the agenda controls the meeting.

The most effective agendas are public and written down. If the agenda remains unclear to the whole group, the meeting may be hijacked by private agendas.

The final responsibility for setting the agenda is the Chair's. After all, it's the Chair who is calling the meeting. If you are the Chair, involve your administrator. You will not be able to function efficiently unless you delegate at least some of the administration of the meeting, and the administrator will not be able to contribute fully if not kept in the picture.

Keep it simple. The more difficult it is to organise the agenda, the greater the likelihood that the meeting will be unproductive.

Why have an agenda?

A written agenda allows everyone to focus on what they are to do before, during and after the meeting. It acts as:

- a plan of the meeting to aid preparation;
- an objective control of the meeting's progress;
- a measure of the meeting's success.

If you already have a written agenda, can you improve it in any way? If you don't, it's not too late to write one! A single piece of paper including the matters you wish to deal with, or a list on a flipchart, is better than nothing.

The word 'agenda' is Latin for 'things to be done'. An agenda should not be a list of subject headings. Each agenda item should be an instruction. It should tell the participants:

- what the task is;
- how it will be tackled;
- what the group will do at the end of the item.

Every item on the agenda should contain at least one verb, indicating what the group will *do*. 'Item 7: New IT network' says very little that will help participants to prepare. Verbs give a clear indication of what kind of action you are expecting at that point in the meeting.

'Item 3: New IT network. Clive *to present* quotations and essential specifications of systems under consideration. Team *to agree* system to be recommended for purchase.' This much fuller entry indicates what the group is to do, who has a key responsibility in carrying out the task, and how we will know whether we have achieved our objective.

Here is a checklist of what most formal agendas will include (in this order):

- Title of meeting

- Date, time, venue
- Apologies for absence
- Minutes of previous meeting
- Matters arising from the previous meeting
- Other items to be discussed and decided
- Motions relating to the above
- Reports from sub-committees
- Contributions from guest speakers
- Any other business
- Date, time and venue of next meeting

Your agenda may not need to be so comprehensive. Consider the advantages of including timings for each item and 'owners' for each item.

Constructing the agenda

As you gather items for the agenda, look for:

- a logical order;
- a common thread: keep linked items together;
- routine items: place near the beginning;
- special factors (for example, people who are only involved in a part of the meeting);
- difficult or contentious items.

The agenda should follow a natural shape. The most 'difficult' items – those needing the most discussion and thinking work – will be best placed in the middle third of the meeting, when the group's physical and mental alertness are at their peak. Routine items, information items or urgent matters that can be dealt with quickly, can be put first; and the 'easiest' items – those of greatest interest, or presentations by guest speakers – towards the end.

The agenda should also reflect the thinking process that you wish to follow. Very few agendas pay any real attention to the type of thinking that different objectives require. Problem solving, evaluation of information and conflict resolution, for example, will all need different approaches. Groups at different stages of a project, or meeting for the first time, will think in different ways.

Every group thinking task will probably move through three broad stages.

1. *Evidence* – gathering, collating and organising information about the matter.
2. *Interpretation* – what we think about the evidence, different perspectives and implications.
3. *Action* – what our interpretation suggests we might do.

Be careful to illustrate these stages in your agenda, in whatever way is appropriate to the task in hand. People may try to jump between stages, confusing evidence with interpretation or suggesting action before interpretation is complete. Making the stages clear in the agenda itself will help you to manage the group's thinking more effectively.

Here is a checklist of the essentials when assembling the items on your agenda:

- Remove any unnecessary items.
- Give detailed titles to each item.
- Every title should contain at least one verb: what the group will do.
- Give timings to each item.
- Indicate any specific speakers to an item.
- Note any attached papers, in case they get lost.
- Consider putting motions on a separate sheet, for ease of reference.

Beware 'Any other business'! If something is worth discussing, it should be itemised on the agenda. All too often, people use 'AOB' to pursue private or hidden agendas, to settle old scores, reawaken old grudges or make lengthy and irrelevant complaints. If you can, remove this item from the agenda. Remember that your meeting should end on a positive note, with a summary of what you have achieved and the suggested next steps.

You can avoid 'any other business' by:

- distributing a draft agenda, with invitations for contributions;
- inviting participants to submit any late business at the start of the meeting;
- deciding whether to include extra items, on the basis of their urgency, not their importance. Make it clear that any late inclusions are at the Chair's discretion;
- amending the agenda. Consider placing the new items at the beginning of the meeting, rather than at the end;
- allocating time to the new items and revising the timings for the rest of the agenda. Keep to the original overall timing of the meeting; simply extending it is counterproductive.

Watching the clock

Some Chairs seem to make it a point of honour to have meetings that last for hours. But a successful meeting depends on how well everybody participates, not on how long it is.

No meeting, or part of a meeting, should last longer than 90 minutes. Many meetings must last longer for logistical reasons: it's expensive to gather a group from far and wide into one room. But, if the meeting must last longer, build in break times, with suitable refreshments. Above all, set a time to finish.

Announce it on the agenda – and stick to it! It is, at the very least, bad manners not to.

Less is more. *Fit the items on the agenda to the available time* – and not the other way around. A group can perform well only for so long: the more you try to pack on to your agenda, the less you will achieve. Timings for individual items are useful here: if you find you can allocate only a few minutes to an important item, you are overfilling the agenda. Always be on the lookout, too, for unnecessary items, which can be dealt with outside the meeting.

You can make your meeting shorter in the following way:

- Announce a finishing time. It's discourteous not to.
- Limit the number of items on the agenda to the time allowed.
- Allocate a task owner to each item, who will take responsibility for any decision.
- Impose a time limit on each agenda item.
- Allow time for breaks.
- Prepare procedures for unresolved business.
- Make it your goal to end on time!

5

Chairing the meeting

Chairing a meeting is essentially a leadership task. The Chair's task is to release the talents of the group. You should provide:

- *vision:* what the meeting is aiming for;
- *direction:* indicating where to go;
- *security:* developing the group's well-being and sense of purpose.

How you do this will depend very much on the style of chairing that you find congenial. The best Chairs wear their authority lightly. Lao-tsu, the writer of the *Tao Te Ching* recognised this over 2,000 years ago:

> The best soldier is not soldierly
> The best fighter is not ferocious
> The best conqueror does not take part in the war
> The best employer of men keeps himself below them
> This is called the virtue of not contending
> This is called the ability of using people.

'The best conqueror does not take part in the war.' This sums up good chairing. Direct the process of the meeting; delegate task leadership to participants. Lead the operation; but don't take part.

Leadership in meetings

What sort of leader do you intend to be? Try to be clear about how you will conduct the meeting before you begin. What type of meeting is it? Does it have regulations or legal requirements governing the way it is run? How do you expect participants to contribute? How will you control procedure? Will everybody address their remarks formally through the Chair? Perhaps you will opt for a strategy of minimal control: announcing each item, summarising discussion, calling for a formal decision – and keeping to time.

One of the most common criticisms of Chairs is that they fail to control the meeting. Another is that they are too autocratic! Strict control must be exercised at the start of the meeting, when a group is newly formed, or when the meeting is large and a high degree of procedural discipline must be invoked. 'Strong' control is useful in a crisis, or to get through routine items quickly. Otherwise a democratic style is preferable. Groups work best when they feel ownership of the tasks to be undertaken, and empowered to act. They will also work more efficiently if they feel secure: that somebody is in overall control.

Opening the meeting

A meeting that starts badly will take time to recover. It is a good idea to work out an opening procedure in some detail: it will steady the nerves and put everybody at ease. You should:

- Start on time. If you do not, you will have late arrivals for the next meeting. Lateness can become a chronic problem if not dealt with immediately. Anybody who arrives late at a meeting that started promptly should soon get the message.

- State the purpose or objective of the meeting. Refer to the agenda, and indicate the common ground that exists within the group to reach this goal.
- Make all suitable introductions. Check that everybody knows each other. Attend in particular to new members.
- Announce procedures and the timetable of the meeting. Tell people how long the meeting will last, and times of breaks. Indicate how you expect them to contribute and how discussion will be controlled.
- If you are chairing a new group:
  - identify and agree the group's purpose;
  - give information on everybody attending: their expertise and relevance to the task;
  - invite everybody to introduce themselves.
- If the group is well established:
  - identify the purpose of *this* meeting;
  - note any changes in circumstances since the last meeting;
  - remind the group of its identity;
  - introduce new members or guests;
  - praise achievements of the group or individuals since the last meeting;
  - acknowledge new difficulties;
  - reaffirm the determination of the meeting to meet the challenge.

Managing agenda items

Lead by example. Keep the group focused on your vision of the meeting: not only what we want to achieve, but how we want to behave. Manage the conversation by asking questions, listening, energising, praising, accepting and, occasionally, disciplining. Check that the task leader is satisfied with the outcome: that decisions and actions, and the responsibilities and deadlines associated with them, are clear.

Take each item separately, and in order. Clarify which item the meeting is addressing, and redirect participants when they stray into other items:

- Refer to the agenda.
- Do not start an item before concluding the previous one.
- Clarify the purpose of the item.
- Start the discussion positively.
- Remind the group how much time is allocated.
- Give any relevant background information.
- Try to change your approach from item to item.

Ensure that the meeting does not waste time. Be ready to check whether the discussion is useful to the task leader, or even necessary. Challenge gossip, in particular. Remind participants of their responsibilities to use time well. You might even record the time taken for each item against the task leader's name: this can work wonders for group discipline!

Encouraging contributions

Most of us sometimes need to be encouraged to speak out. An important idea may never emerge because somebody is too reticent or overawed to volunteer it. Meetings can easily become 'tennis matches' dominated by a few strong personalities while everybody else looks on helplessly. The Chair can encourage democracy in two ways – by *task behaviour*: initiating discussion, building on it, making suggestions; and by *process behaviour*: gate-keeping to allow everyone to contribute; time-keeping to concentrate people's minds; and summarising the group's feelings.

Everybody should feel relaxed about contributing, and that their contribution is valued. Distinguish contributions from the people making them. Praise useful ideas and remarks rather than according the speaker gushing adoration; be critical, if you must, of a comment without condemning the speaker. Be open, honest and *specific*:

- Always ask for different points of view.
- Note which people are not talking and make space for them to contribute.
- Discipline more dominant group members.
- Separate different stages of the conversation – and keep the distinctions clear.
- Separate creative contributions from critical ones.

Using questions and statements

At the next meeting you attend, count the number of questions. Compare it to the number of assertions made. What conclusions can you draw?

Managers are often dismayed at the lack of questions in meetings they chair. Perhaps they have forgotten how politically charged questions – or being seen to question – can be. In many organisations, to question is simply 'not done'. 'Questioning,' wrote Samuel Johnson with typically heavy irony, 'is not the mode of conversation among gentlemen.' As a result, many managers become much more skilled in advocating their own ideas than in enquiring into those of others – or into their own.

We ask questions to:

- find out;
- check our understanding;
- help others improve their understanding;
- invite others to question our thinking;
- make requests for action or information.

Of course, we also use questions for many other reasons, such as to:

- accentuate the difference between our ideas and those of others;
- ridicule or make somebody look foolish;
- criticise;
- find fault or flaws;
- make us look clever;
- express our position 'politically': in relation to an alliance, to a subgroup or to the group as a whole;
- trip somebody up;
- force the speaker into a corner;
- disguise a statement of opinion;
- create an adversarial situation.

If we are not getting the answers we want, we have not asked the right questions.

Become aware of the repertoire of questions available to you. Use them to help you pilot the conversation: to open it, keep it alive, take it in new directions, steer it away from dangerous waters or shallows where it might get stuck, and bring it to a close.

Ask genuine questions, truly seeking information, encouraging people to speak from their experience and expertise, rather than 'putting answers into their mouths'.

Types of question

Closed (can only be answered 'yes' or 'no')	*'Can you...? ' 'Will you...?' 'Is it...?' 'Do you...?'*	Gets a 'yes' or 'no' Establishes matters of fact Focuses the discussion Stops rambling Checks understanding

Open (cannot be answered 'yes' or 'no')	*'Why/what/who/where/ when/how?'*	Avoids 'yes' or 'no' Opens up discussion Encourages a contribution Gains information in a non-directive way Gets ideas
Specific	*'At what point...?'* *'Where exactly...?'*	Directs the discussion Prevents rambling Engages expertise Brings people into the conversation Speeds up and focuses attention
Overhead	*'What do we all think?'*	Addresses the group Helps to avoid embarrassment Stimulates answers from newcomers Can help to make a point without sacrificing impartiality
Relay	*'Thanks Nadeem. Tony, what do you think?'*	From one speaker to another Comparing ideas Keeping the conversation moving
Reverse	*Well: what do you think?'*	Reflects a question back to questioner Encourages a speaker to expand or qualify

Statements are useful at the beginning of a meeting, to define the purpose, objectives and scope of the conversation. Be sure to make any opening statement positive. Statements during items of a meeting can be used to:

- *introduce it:* 'We're all aware of the problems in this area. They include…';
- *give information:* 'This is a new venture for the company. Briefly it works like this...';
- *temper conflict or confusion with fact:* 'Perhaps I can make a few points clear at this stage...';
- *gauge the mood of the group:* 'I can see that there's a good deal of frustration about this...', 'I think we're all satisfied with that decision...', 'It seems to me that we're getting confused...';
- *provoke, to energise or stimulate discussion:* 'Our jobs all depend on this!'

Summarising

All meetings go through periods of relative calm, between or within items. The group is uncertain of the next move: the conversation dries up, begins to go in circles or degenerates into chat. At times like this, the Chair should intervene with a summary.

Good timing is essential. Don't try to summarise when the discussion is in full swing: take notes to prepare yourself for the moment when the group stops generating ideas. There are three main points in any meeting when summarising becomes a useful tool to guide the conversation:

1. *Summarising within items.* Control contributions by summarising them: when they ramble, repeat themselves or become anecdotal. Mark the end of one phase of the conversation with a summary before inviting further comments. Summarise to bring together the strands of a discussion, or when it goes slack. Sometimes a summary can be used to check how much agreement you have achieved and to reopen the discussion.

2. *Summarising at the end of items.* This will seal an agreement or clarify exactly what has been agreed. This is a task that can usefully be given to the administrator, to help clarify what to put in the minutes.
3. *Summarising at the end of the meeting.* A brief summary will remind the group of its achievement and point the way forward to the actions that will be taken.

Problem people

Every meeting has them. A group member becomes a problem if his or her individual interests come into conflict with those of the group. A basic rule is to treat problem people as members of the group, and not as troublesome individuals. This may be easier said than done!

Problem people and how to deal with them

The bulldog

Aggressive, inflexible Looking for a fight Out to score points Liable to attack without warning	Give him a bone to chew Separate his words from his manner Keep cool

The horse

Keen but boring Goes by the book Intelligent but could plod on forever	Lead them to water: give them a job to do Harness their remarks by summarising and restating

The fox

Crafty Undermines the meeting Conspiratorial, whispers a lot A potential hijacker	Force them to make their views public Look for the hidden agenda Set the bulldog on them

The monkey	
Know-it-all	Keep control of procedure
Point-of-order expert	Ask closed questions
Chatters incessantly	Give them something to do
Swings from 'tree to tree'	
Volunteers a lot	
The hedgehog	
Prickly	Tickle their bellies
Whines and whinges	Respect their expertise
Despises everybody else: may have been squashed once or twice	Ask them to help
Sceptical, unhelpful, defensive (curls into a ball)	Give them status
The gazelle	
Timid and retiring	Ask direct questions
May be young	Encourage
Liable to run away	Praise
A silent worrier	Seduce into the conversation
Unwilling to stand their ground	Protect from bulldogs
The frog	
Blabbermouth	Keep to the point
Leaps in unthinkingly	Appeal to the clock
'Read it, read it'	Ignore their gaffes
Ill-informed	Ask them to do the minutes
Puts his foot in it: potential victim of the fox	
The hippo	
Wallows	Try to heave them out of the mud
Half asleep	Pick on them suddenly
Likes mud, and not much else	Challenge them
Will agree to anything	
Likely to say: 'Why me?'	
The giraffe	
Easily distracted	Bring them down to earth
Dreams in the treetops	Show respect
Rather sensitive	Don't trip them up
Will do anything not to fall over	Seduce into the conversation
A silent worrier	Protect from bulldogs
Unwilling to stand their ground	

Difficult situations

The meeting that goes exactly according to plan probably doesn't exist. If the Chair and participants are behaving professionally, few situations should cause major disruption. The following are perhaps the most serious and the most common.

conflict

Conflict is undoubtedly one of the most common sources of anxiety in meetings. Many meetings seem to collapse into argument, hostility and ritual recrimination almost as a matter of course. Do not regard conflict as inevitable or desirable. You are not powerless in the face of emotional hostility but, in order to handle it well, you need to distance yourself from it.

Begin by trying to locate the source of the problem. Sometimes this is obvious: insecurity at a time of great change, stress, a new set of working relationships or pressure from public exposure. On other occasions, conflict may seem to bubble up from nowhere, starting with something small and escalating quickly as it takes hold of the group. Conflict thrives on confusion and doubt. Some group members may seek to manipulate it for their own ends or use it to justify their cynicism about all matters managerial. As conflict grows through a group, it becomes more emotional, generalised and unfocused. Looking for a target, it can find the Chair, turning the meeting into an all-purpose 'grouse session'.

Hostility often results from a sense of powerlessness. It is the feeling of being at the mercy of forces outside our control that is so disabling. This is why anger often centres on what has happened in the past, and in particular on what 'they' have done: senior management, other teams, department heads, rogue operators who have bucked the system, engineers or sales staff who are never in the office, customers, suppliers, competitors... Be prepared. If you are facing conflict or group resistance, you must give yourself a single overriding objective: to empower the group to do something practical. Only by focusing their thoughts on the future, and on what they can do, will you *transform* people's energy from conflict into purposeful activity. Arm yourself with some guiding principles:

- Make the objective of the meeting clear at the outset. Write it up on a flipchart and be ready to refer back to it frequently. Challenge people to explain the relevance of their remarks to the meeting's objectives.
- Remember that your task is to control the conversation. Resist being drawn into the emotional maelstrom, however hard that may be.
- Slow the conversation down. Do not mirror the tone, pitch or speed of others' speech.
- Do not interrupt – or cut people off in mid-sentence.
- Listen and record the points people make. A flipchart or whiteboard is often a powerful way to focus the conversation on one area and can defuse conflict effectively.
- Don't join in. Do not be tempted to argue, or to contradict opinions or generalisations: about what 'they' do, or what 'always' happens. A good response to such remarks would be: 'In what circumstances does this happen?'
- Turn complaints into objectives. Ask people to restate them as 'how to' statements. Write these up on the flipchart and display them.
- Stop people from talking about others who are not at the meeting. Insist that 'they' are not here and we are, and that only we can address our objectives.
- Focus on solutions, not problems. Think forwards, not back – and encourage the group to do the same.
- Be a broken record! Repeat your questions to the group, over and over – 'What are we trying to do? What can *we* do about it? How does this relate to our objectives?'

- Be specific. People should know what contribution they are being asked to make, and how their contribution will fit in to wider objectives. Being explicit about goals and targets is the only way to achieve this. If you genuinely consult – ask for suggestions, invite people to participate in finding solutions – a great deal of resistance will melt away.
- Focus on *action*. Draw the group's attention away from what others have done or are doing towards *what we will do in the future*. You will have to be sensitive about this. Demonstrating that you understand people's grievances can be useful in winning them over to your own ideas, and in rooting out areas for improvement. However, there will come a point in a 'grouse session' when you should start asking, insistently but quietly: 'So what are we going to do?' In this way, you will divert attention from damaging 'storytelling' and complaint towards commitment and agreement. By showing that something can be done, you can show people that they have power to change things.

Hidden agendas

We all go to meetings with our own private agendas. They may emerge or remain hidden. They are only harmful when they come into conflict with the meeting's public agenda.

Good private agendas might include:

- seeing the meeting as a career investment;
- helping the Chair to achieve a successful meeting;
- strengthening the group;
- encouraging other participants;
- gaining agreement for your own plans.

Bad private agendas include:

- wanting to please;
- empire building;
- wanting to conform;
- venting your frustration;
- causing conflict;
- discrediting a rival;
- undermining the Chair;
- scoring points off others;
- riding a favourite hobbyhorse;
- demonstrating how overworked you are ('Poor me...').

Evidence of harmful hidden agendas might include:

- stonewalling ('I've no choice', delay, promises unfulfilled, outright refusal to act);
- attack (on every idea and everybody: insults, bullying, lots of bluster);
- trickery (denying having said something, twisting an argument, double meanings).

Some hidden agendas are truly Machiavellian, ruled by expediency, craft and cunning. Many more are the result of fear: of having to commit to an action we would rather not take, or of opposition if we were to make the hidden agenda public.

The most dangerous thing about a hidden agenda is that it is hidden. If you can locate the fear that causes it, you may be able to remove the agenda by removing the fear. If you cannot trace suspicious tactics to their source, you may be able at least to show that you recognise the tactic. This may stop the behaviour recurring, though it may not root out the hidden agenda itself.

Do not let your suspicions become paranoia. In turning the search for hidden agendas into a witch-hunt, you will start to create your own hidden agenda.

Power games and politics

Politics are an inevitable part of our lives as members of groups. All meetings will therefore involve politics of some kind. Getting things done means wielding power. Wielding power alone, of course, does not ensure that anything useful is achieved! In some cases, calling a meeting is a sign merely that somebody has acquired enough power to call a meeting. Power games and politics express tensions and shifting relationships within the group. If you chair meetings, you will find yourself involved in political behaviour.

You must decide how you propose to deal with it. How do you seek to influence others? What kinds of power do you have and which would you like to cultivate? How do those around you use power? How can you influence those with influence, so as to align them with your objectives?

Hijacking

Hijacking is a severe loss of direction, which occurs when a private agenda attempts to take over. It may even involve a conspiracy.

The Chair and participants have a duty to rescue the meeting from hijacking. Alliances may need to be made and appeals made to the agenda. A hijack by definition is by one person or a minority. Appeals to group solidarity should be sufficient to solve the problem, at least temporarily. An attempted hijack usually means that a major issue needs to be addressed: a period of storming may ensue.

Senior management are liable to hijack meetings chaired by subordinates. The Chair must exercise proper authority. If the meeting is conducted properly and fairly, they will have nothing to fear from a responsible senior manager – who may after all be assessing their leadership potential.

Groupthink

In the 1960s, Irving Janis studied a number of disastrous US foreign policy decisions, including the Bay of Pigs. He attributed these poor decisions to a phenomenon he labelled 'groupthink'. Janis (1968) defined groupthink as 'the psychological drive for consensus at any cost that suppresses dissent and appraisal of alternatives in cohesive decision-making groups'.

Groupthink results from a group's pursuit of social cohesion. Group members self-censor contributions that the group might interpret as 'deviant' from its norms; as a result, the meeting's thinking becomes dangerously limited to what the group allows. Symptoms of groupthink include the illusion of invulnerability and an unthinking sense of unanimity. The consequences can be a severe limitation of thinking in the meeting, a misjudgement of risk and wilfully ignoring alternative points of view.

To counteract groupthink:

- challenge the need for collective decision making and appoint 'decision owners'; encourage diverse opinions systematically;
- appoint one person in the group as 'devil's advocate', to evaluate all contributions critically;
- pursue disagreements in an orderly way;
- invite outsiders or new group members to 'kick-start' change;
- ensure that the task leader or process director is willing to have his or her own judgements examined critically;
- examine the procedures of the group: how often you meet; how long since you changed personnel; whether you act democratically.

Closing the meeting

Closing the meeting well is as important as opening it. The group is about to disperse. We must show it what it has achieved in terms of its tasks and objectives.

Delegate as many actions as possible. This will:

- relieve you of some of the burden;
- give ownership of actions to participants;
- demonstrate trust; and
- build the team.

All agreed actions should have a named 'actioner'. Actioners should feel that they 'own' the action: they should understand why they are doing it and have the authority and resources to carry it through. Make sure that nobody takes on an unrealistic amount of work. Schedule actions to happen as soon as possible. Participants are more likely to take prompt action if they are still fired with enthusiasm by the meeting they have just left!

Back up all decisions and actions in writing. A summary action sheet distributed with (or before) the full minutes can be useful. Others affected by the action may need to be contacted by memo or e-mail. You should:

- Summarise what has been decided and point the way ahead.
- Briefly announce what actions are to be taken, by whom and when.
- Test for commitment.
- Check that the administrator is happy with the record of the meeting.
- Set the time and date of the next meeting if possible.
- End positively. Emphasise the achievements of the meeting.
- Thank everybody for their attendance and their contributions.

You may think that the meeting is over as soon as it finishes. But there will usually be more to do. The minutes, for one thing, will need to be produced. Do you have an efficient process for issuing them? And most actions will need to be followed up at the appropriate time. If 'actioners' have not done what they committed to by the agreed deadline, you may need to do more than complain. Ask why things have not been done. Maybe the actioner was over-enthusiastic and took on too much; maybe the action itself was unrealistic.

Meetings are rarely single events. Often, they are part of a cycle of activity: a meeting leads to action, which provokes change, which itself must be evaluated or responded to – usually by calling another meeting! As the Chair, your responsibility for holding successful meetings is almost certainly closely connected to your wider responsibilities as a manager and leader. It is in meetings that you have the opportunity to exercise those responsibilities publicly.

6

Conversation: the heart of the meeting

At the heart of any meeting is conversation. It is by conversing that we express our thinking and relationships to each other. If we want to improve our meetings, we must improve the quality of the conversations that take place in them.

The dynamics of conversation

Conversation is a verbal dance. The word, from Latin, has the root meaning of 'to keep turning with'. Conversation relies for its success on all participants moving in their thinking.

Like any dance, conversation has rules and standard moves. These allow people to move more harmoniously together, without stepping on each other's toes. Different kinds of conversation have different conventions. Some are implicitly understood; others must be spelt out in detail and rehearsed.

This sense of a conversation is well expressed in the word 'dialogue'. The purpose of dialogue (from the Greek, 'meaning through') is to construct a new, shared meaning through conversation: a meaning that would not come into being if the conversation did not happen. We explore each other's perceptions, offer our own for examination and transform our thinking in the light of others'. This, at its very best, is what conversation can achieve.

Talking and listening

The dynamic of conversation involves two elements: talking and listening. These two activities do not happen merely in sequence, but simultaneously: each participant in a conversation is both speaker and listener *throughout the conversation.*

Most of us are better at talking than at listening. As managers, we are trained in the techniques of presenting, explaining and influencing. Our education mostly stresses the value of *arguing*: taking a position, holding it, defending it, convincing others of its worth and attacking any argument that threatens it. As a result, our conversations tend not to dance but to push and shove.

Dialogue or debate?

In an attempt to impose order on our conversations, we have invented *debate* (from the Latin, 'to beat down').

Debate is probably the only kind of disciplined conversation that any of us have learnt. In a debate, two ideas are set against each other. Each idea tries to discredit the other. The idea left standing at the end of the debate is presumed to be correct. For debate to be effective, we must manage our ideas very strictly. Only two can be allowed at a time; the two ideas chosen must be opposed in some way.

Why is debate so common a form of conversation? Partly, because we are familiar with the idea of an argument. Debate seems to make sense of our seemingly natural ability to argue. Most of us find arguing uncomfortable but unavoidable. Somehow, we dislike it but can't stop ourselves doing it. Debate allows us to argue without getting too injured. Instead of enduring a verbal brawl, we set up a boxing match.

Much is made in management theory of the virtue of debate. It is said to be not merely unavoidable in business, but positively desirable: a recent article in *Harvard Business Review* calls it 'creative abrasion'. No less an authority than Peter Drucker (1979) has written: 'the understanding that underlies the right decision grows out of the clash and conflict of divergent opinions and out of the serious consideration of competing alternatives'.

Yet debate, with its clash of divergent opinions, makes it impossible for us to consider the competing alternatives seriously. After all, *neither* idea might be correct; *both* may be partially correct. There may be lots of other ideas that might be valuable to consider. There may be no 'correct' idea in the context of the conversation. We may not even be trying to find the correct answer, but looking for new ideas or workable solutions to an insoluble problem. Debate cannot allow us to consider any of these possibilities – or any others that we might be able to think of. We are too busy trying to prove the opposing idea wrong to consider either idea seriously. Often, we are too busy defending ourselves, too frightened to venture from our corner, too battle-fatigued.

A debate is a conflict of rigid opinions. Opinions are ideas gone cold. They are our assumptions about what might, or should, be true rather than what is true in specific circumstances. They may take the form of:

- *stories* (about what happened, what may have happened, why it may have happened);
- *explanations* (of why something went wrong, or why we failed);
- *justifications* (for taking action or not);

- *wrong-making* (I am right, you are wrong);
- *gossip* (to make us feel better at the expense of others);
- *generalisations* (to save us the trouble of thinking).

We are so used to voicing and listening to opinions that we can easily mistake them for the truth. Whenever you hear the word 'fact' in a meeting, you can be almost certain that somebody is voicing an opinion.

It is unusual for any meeting to avoid adversarial thinking. It usually appears in one of four forms.

Critical thinking

For most of us, to think about something is automatically to look for something wrong with it. Take note next time you ask anybody for their response to an issue: invariably their first thoughts will be critical.

The rationale behind critical thinking is that, by looking for the weaknesses in an idea, we can strengthen it. But we rarely receive criticism in this way; instead, we try to defend our idea from the criticism or attack the criticism itself, in an effort to discredit it.

Ego thinking

In adversarial thinking, we become identified with our ideas. Criticism of an idea quickly becomes an attack on the person holding it. Debate is used as a pretext for scoring points against others. Reason gets infected with emotion.

Meetings often devote enormous amounts of energy to preventing emotion from overwhelming debate, but the dynamic of debate makes emotional conflict inevitable.

Rigid thinking

All thinking starts from assumptions. We can't think without first assuming something. Debate merely pits these assumptions against each other. Because they are assumed, they are rarely stated – which makes them difficult to challenge or knock down. Whoever wins the debate, the assumptions lying behind the ideas will survive – on *both* sides. This makes our thinking rigid. Any thinking that questions an assumption, or strays beyond its boundaries, can be dismissed as 'irrelevant' (or 'deviant'). Indeed, debate actually serves to *entrench* assumptions – and thereby prolong the conflict.

Rigid thinking is often the result of:

- conforming to authority ('if senior management see it this way, it must be right');
- the influence of custom ('our profession has thought like this for the last 200 years');
- habit ('this is the way we think around here');
- wilful ignorance ('thinking like this saves us the bother of dealing with inconvenient detail or finding out more').

Political thinking

Political thinking connects ideas to the people holding them. Once an idea becomes identified with an individual, we realise that winning the debate means allying ourselves to the person as well as the idea. To attack an idea is to attack its sponsor; to support it is to create an alliance. We begin to use conversational gambits, ploys, manoeuvres and defence mechanisms, not to develop the conversation but to play politics: creating 'power bases' and undermining 'opponents', bureaucratic conniving, behind-the-scenes manipulation and rumour-mongering.

We accord debate enormous prestige. We train it in our

schools – indeed it is probably the only kind of disciplined conversation we ever train our children to conduct. We perpetuate debate in the media, where issues are explored by setting two 'experts' against each other for the cameras. We even allow ourselves to be governed largely through debate. It's no wonder that managers try to become adept in the skills of debating. Whoever can defend their ideas in the boardroom and withstand the onslaught of their peers – or, better still, their superiors – gains high status and may even be promoted on the basis of their 'strong character'. They become 'heroes' and the stuff of myth.

Adversarial thinking is self-perpetuating. Like other kinds of conflict, it is cyclical and can escalate easily. Being attacked for our ideas causes pain; we respond in kind and help to prolong the conflict. We may engage in 'pre-emptive strikes', attacking before being attacked. Adversarial thinking expresses our lack of security, and the need to protect ourselves from future threats. We become locked in a 'Cold War' of argument and counter-argument. Although we may recognise that our behaviour is unproductive, we feel we cannot do anything different. We do not know how to, and we may be too frightened to try.

Beyond adversarial thinking

How, then, can we break out of the vicious spiral? What can we do to help meetings evolve beyond the fruitless and exhausting ritual of adversarial thinking? Perhaps the first step is to improve our listening.

The gentle art of listening

The quality of any conversation depends on the quality of the listening. Listening is far more than simply not speaking. The listener controls the speaker's behaviour by his or her own: by maintaining or breaking eye contact, by body position, by nodding or shaking his or her head, by taking notes or doodling, and so on. Similarly, when we speak, we demonstrate the quality of our listening. If we interrupt, we demonstrate that we have stopped listening, that we are not interested in listening any longer. This, in turn, will affect the other's speaking and listening. We all know the symptoms of poor listening. They are so familiar that we even expect them and develop tactics to cope with them. They include:

- outright condemnation of an idea;
- criticising the speaker's delivery;
- only replying to a part of what somebody has said;
- interrupting;
- daydreaming;
- paying attention to a distraction;
- holding another conversation at the same time;
- evading the issue;
- using emotional words;
- going to sleep.

Most of us, however, can listen effectively. We do listen well when we:

- like or admire the speaker;
- want to trip them up;
- think they have something interesting to say;
- expect to be rewarded or punished for listening well;
- know that we will be asked to comment;
- have an overwhelming need to listen;
- are not distracted;
- know or have learnt that effective listening improves group behaviour and leads to improved results in the meeting.

The first step in improving our listening skills is to become aware of the obstacles. Some we have control over, others we may have to endure. Any conversation consists, for each participant, of *two* conversations: the external conversation and the internal conversation we hold inside our own heads. We must listen to both, and take note of both. As we participate in the external conversation, we may be using our internal conversation to:

- suggest answers to problems;
- develop solutions;
- rehearse our next remark;
- judge what the speaker is saying;
- concentrate on a part of what the speaker is saying;
- compare ideas to others we already have;
- plan how to win;
- think about how we can make the speaker like us more;
- congratulate ourselves on being cleverer than the speaker;
- ask what is happening elsewhere in the room;
- dream about something completely different.

At times, we should resolutely *stop* holding our inner conversation and listen – truly listen – to what the speaker is saying, to what he or she is not saying, and how he or she is saying or not saying it. At others, we can manage the internal conversation by:

- taking notes of our thoughts so that we can put them to one side;
- making it part of the external conversation by vocalising our thoughts;
- pausing before we speak, to allow the internal conversation to happen.

Managing the inner conversation will allow us to listen more actively in the external conversation.

Improving the meeting's thinking

Conversation is the way we think together in the meetings we hold. We are paid to think. Our success depends on our results; we think when we want results that are better than they would be without thinking. And yet most of us are not trained to think. Thinking is not yet regarded as a key managerial skill. As a result, we have developed a number of damaging misconceptions about thinking.

- *Thinking is not an alternative to doing.* We can use thinking as an excuse not to act, and we can act without thinking. The reason we do both so much is that we regard thinking and action as opposed. They are not. Effective thinking improves the effectiveness of our actions; and our actions are a rich source of good ideas.
- *Thinking is not intelligence.* Thinking unintelligently may still achieve something. Intelligence without thinking is useless.
- *Thinking is not a function of education.* Highly educated people are not necessarily good thinkers; and many people with little education can think extremely effectively.
- *Thinking is not being clever.* An increase of knowledge is not thinking: it is simply hoarding. Too much information can seriously hamper our ability to think.
- *Thinking is not only the operation of logic.* It involves looking, exploring, choosing, designing, evaluating and having hunches. It includes considering priorities, objectives, alternatives, consequences and other people's opinions.

There is a Japanese proverb: 'None of us is as smart as all of us.' Yet most groups of people think far less well than any one of them individually. Why is this?

We tend to confuse conversation about the task with conversation about process. We identify thoughts with people. We talk in code. We use conversation to express loyalties or alliances, to bid for power, to protect our position or sense of self-worth. We persist in old conventions or habits of conversation to feel more comfortable.

We also fail to manage the structure of the conversation. A well-managed conversation will begin with clear objectives and end with clear actions. Many conversations have unclear agendas (or hidden agendas); others are combinations of several conversations at once. We allow our conversations to ramble, to get stuck, to be hijacked or stifled. Because the behavioural or 'political' aspects of conversation are so powerful, we find it difficult to influence the course of conversations productively – particularly in a meeting, when a group of people are involved.

Tackling these two failings is critically important if we want to help ourselves and others to think better in meetings.

Thinking 'hats'

Serious conversations should seek to distinguish ideas from people. Edward de Bono's (1993) 'Six Thinking Hats' are becoming increasingly popular as tools for clarifying this distinction.

The hats are an example of what de Bono calls 'directed attention thinking tools'. They are a tool to allow us to *direct* our attention to a specific kind of thinking at will. De Bono suggests that we label every contribution to a conversation by means of a coloured 'hat' that the speaker is 'wearing' as they make it. Chairs can also ask participants deliberately to make contributions 'wearing' a particular hat. The six 'hats' are:

- White hat: facts and figures.
- Red hat: emotion, feelings, hunches and intuition.
- Black hat: caution, judgement, fitting propositions to facts.
- Yellow hat: advantages, benefits, savings.
- Green hat: creativity, new ideas, exploration, suggestions.
- Blue hat: thinking about thinking, control of the thinking process, 'points of order'.

The thinking hats create a simple and immediate discipline for our conversations. The beauty of de Bono's hats is that we can put them on and take them off very easily. It would be utterly inappropriate to suggest that someone is a 'red-hat thinker' or a 'black-hat thinker'. Anybody can use the hats whenever they want. Indeed, using the hats allows people to make remarks that they might not ordinarily risk making.

We can use the hats informally or systematically. Judging which hat to pick at which point can become a sophisticated chairing skill in itself.

The two stages of thinking

We can imagine thinking as a process in two stages.

First-stage thinking is concerned with perception: we recognise something because it fits into some pre-existing mental pattern. We can call these mental patterns 'ideas'. Ideas are arrangements of experience in our minds. They allow us to make sense of our experiences; they are the means by which we *have* experiences. In first-stage thinking, we *encode* experience so that we can use it at the second stage. We *name* an object or event; we translate complex activity into an equation; we simplify a structure by drawing a diagram.

In *second-stage thinking*, we make judgements about our experience by manipulating the code. Having named something as, say, a 'cup', we apply logic, custom and aesthetics to judge its effectiveness as a cup. Having labelled a downturn in sales as 'a marketing problem', we use market research, spreadsheets, past experience and critical scrutiny of the marketing department to judge how best to solve it.

Managing our thinking begins by:

- separating the two stages of thinking;
- becoming conscious of which stage we are in at any point;
- applying only the tools and techniques appropriate to that stage.

We are highly skilled in second-stage thinking. We are taught it at school: we learn verbal and mathematical languages, we are encouraged to analyse, to deduce, to argue and to evaluate. (Debate is a form of second-stage thinking.) We are so good at it that we regard it as the sum total of thinking. IQ (intelligence quotient) is a measure of our ability to manipulate language and symbols. So sophisticated is our second-stage thinking that we can construct computers to do it for us.

We are not nearly so skilled at first-stage thinking. We are taught virtually no techniques to help us improve our perceptions. Yet a change in our first-stage thinking can have dramatic consequences at the second stage. If we decide that the cup is not a cup but a trophy – or a vase, a mug, a chalice – our second-stage thinking about it will change. Our 'marketing problem' may actually be a 'product quality problem', a 'distribution problem', 'a personnel problem', a 'macroeconomic problem' – or a subtle combination of all five.

Second-stage thinking is focused on results. First-stage thinking is not focused at all, and this makes us uncomfortable. Where second-stage thinking is 'deep', concentrating our attention on a single idea, first-stage thinking is 'shallow', directing our attention over a wide area of experience. Second-stage thinking focuses; first-stage thinking scans. First-stage thinking can create anxiety because it delays the moment of deciding, forces us to suspend judgement and challenges our current way of seeing reality. We prefer to take our perceptions for granted, but no amount of good second-stage thinking will be effective if it is based on limited or faulty perceptions. Good thinking pays attention to both stages of the process.

The great Swiss psychologist, Carl Jung (1976), developed the two stages of thinking into two sets of paired complementary functions: *sensation and intuition* at the first stage; *feeling and reasoning* at the second. Jung himself used this model as the basis of a theory of personality types; it may be familiar as the basis of the Myers-Briggs type indicator (see Bayne, 1997).

Using Jung's model, we can formulate the kind of questions we might ask at each stage of the thinking process. First-stage thinking questions include: 'What can we see?' (Sensation), 'What might it mean?' (Intuition). Second-stage questions include: 'What can we do?' (Reasoning), 'What shall we do?' (Feeling).

Four types of conversation

This model suggests four types of conversation that we can use at the different stages of our thinking.

A conversation for relationship

First stage: sensation

Whatever we can accomplish in a meeting is determined by our relationship: what we can say to each other, or ask of each other, is defined by the terms of that relationship. The actions we can commit to are limited by the boundaries of the relationship.

A conversation for relationship is intended to create and generate the relationship necessary to achieve our objectives. It is an exploration. Who are we? How do we relate to the matter in hand? What links us? How do we see things? What do you see that I can't see? What do I see that you don't see? In what ways do we see things similarly, or differently? How can we understand each other? Where do we stand? Can we stand together?

Conversations for relationship are tentative and sometimes awkward: meeting at a social event, or the opening of a job interview, are good examples. Serious conversations for relationship go beyond social conversation or finding common interests. In meetings, this first conversation is often rushed or ignored, simply because it can feel embarrassing.

A conversation for possibility

First stage: intuition

It is in conversations for possibility that first-stage thinking finds its fullest expression. A conversation for possibility is *not* about whether we can do something. It seeks to find new ways of looking at reality. It is a conversation exploring a wide range of perceptions, making distinctions without judging them, looking for something new.

There are a number of ways of doing this: by looking at something from a different angle; by asking for differing interpretations; by distinguishing what we see from our interpretation of it; by distinguishing different people's perceptions. We can isolate one element of a situation and concentrate on it, or relate elements into a larger web of perceptions. We can create metaphors of an issue in order to see it in a radically new light. Conversations for possibility are potentially a source of creativity: brainstorming is a good example.

A conversation for possibility is necessarily a delicate one. Possibility is, by definition, ambiguous; it may be difficult to articulate. For these reasons, conversations for possibility almost never occur unless they are managed. They must be approached with careful thought:

- *Welcome wild ideas.* People must know that they are allowed to speculate, to utter ambiguous, half-formed or crazy ideas.
- *Prohibit second-stage thinking.* Do not allow judgements, criticisms or even analysis of ideas. Listen for the words 'right' or 'wrong'. Possibilities are never right or wrong: they are simply possibilities. For every contribution, ask: 'What's interesting about it?' Encourage the group to build on ideas. Say: 'Yes and...' rather than 'No, but...'.
- *Decide nothing.* Make it clear that no decisions will be taken until this conversation is over: that people are not committing themselves to anything by contributing.
- *Be on the lookout for 'conversations of no possibility':* when people remark that 'this is the way it is and always will be'. Listen for statements of fact and challenge them: 'facts' may be merely well established opinions; they certainly are not possibilities. Challenge, too, statements including words like 'generally', 'usually', 'certainly', 'always'. They are probably assertions of no possibility. Ask: 'In what circumstances?'
- *Challenge opinions or meanings.* Ask: 'What makes you say that?', 'What leads you to that conclusion?' Ask explicitly for alternative interpretations of observations.
- *Challenge the limits of the group's observation* by asking: 'What if...?' or 'How about…?'
- *Manage the emotional quality of the conversation.* Make it clear that you do not welcome inappropriate jokes, personal judgemental comments or emotional 'explosions'. De Bono's Red Hat is useful for allowing people to objectify their emotional responses to ideas; if a response is powerfully negative, challenge people to find what is good about it and remind them that this is a conversation for possibility and nothing more.

A conversation for opportunity

Second stage: thinking

Many of the good ideas that are generated in meetings never become reality because no clear path of opportunity is mapped out. A conversation for opportunity is designed to construct such a path. It is fundamentally a conversation about planning.

Where can we act? What could we do? Which possibilities do we build on? Which are feasible? The bridge from possibility to opportunity is measurement or conditions of satisfaction: targets, milestones, obstacles, and measures of success. How will we be able to judge when we have achieved an objective?

We hold a conversation for opportunity to choose what to do. We assess what we would need to make action possible: resources, support and skills. The group's thinking here is more focused than in a conversation for possibility: in choosing from among a number of possibilities, we are finding a sense of common purpose.

Take care not to kill off possibility by translating it into the detailed plans of opportunity. Keep the spirit of the original idea alive by continually asking: 'What are we trying to achieve?'

Conversations for opportunity can become more imaginative and exciting by placing ourselves in a future where we have achieved our objective. What does such a future look and feel like? What is happening in this imagined future? How can we plan our way towards it? Usually we plan by starting from where we are and extrapolate current actions towards a desired objective. By 'backward planning' from an imagined future, we can find new opportunities for action.

A conversation for action

Second stage: feeling

A conversation for action produces commitment. Translating

opportunity into action requires more than agreement: we need to generate a promise, a commitment to action. That is why this conversation relates to Jung's feeling function. We are asking others to commit with hearts as well as minds. If we take that commitment for granted, we can create anxiety, resentment and pain in others. If we make too many commitments, we can cause ourselves stress.

A conversation for action is a dynamic between requesting and promising:

- I make a request that you do something by a certain time. I must make it clear to you that this is a request, and not an order. Orders may get immediate results; but they are unlikely to get more than the minimum, and they may not achieve results next time.
- You have four possible responses to this request:
  - you may accept;
  - you may decline;
  - you may commit to accept or decline later ('I'll let you know by...');
  - you may make a counter-offer ('No, but I can do something else for you...').
- The conversation based on this request and these responses will result in a promise: 'I will do x for you by time y.'

A meeting will probably contain all four types of conversation: relationship, possibility, opportunity, and action. They will only be truly effective if conducted *in order.*

A conversation's success depends on the success of the conversation preceding it. An unresolved conversation will continue within the next conversation, *in code*. Unresolved aspects of a conversation for relationship can be transformed into hidden agendas or festering 'personality clashes'. Possibilities left unexpressed may become missed opportunities. Above all, if the conversation for action in a meeting does not result in real commitment, we must ask whether we have left any other conversation unfinished.

These four conversations map well on to Tuckman's four-stage model of group development, discussed in Chapter 2. A conversation for relationship is appropriate at the forming stage, when a group is new or responsibilities for tasks are unclear. The storming stage is characterised by conflict between people's perceptions, their versions of reality. A conversation for possibility contains the techniques to take the group through this stage so that it emerges trusting, open and secure. In a conversation for opportunity, the group finds the common purpose and values of the norming stage, focusing on results, choosing a course of action and channelling its thinking into planning. Finally, in a conversation for action, the group is truly performing: exchanging requests and promises honestly and freely, expressing commitment and getting things done.

This integrated model gives us a powerful tool for improving a meeting's thinking. Tuckman offers a useful explanation of group development; Jung suggests the different kinds of thinking that are appropriate at each stage. With a set of conversations to help us manage the four stages, we can begin to combine effective thinking with positive group behaviour – and manage our meetings in a more disciplined way.

7

Participating well

For most of us, the word 'participation' probably suggests how we speak in meetings. But participation is more than making our point well. To participate means to be actively present in the meeting as a member of the group, helping others to participate and contributing to the quality of the thinking within the meeting. Participation is about more than making our voice heard: it is also about helping others to find their voices, and helping the meeting to achieve its objectives.

Enquiry and advocacy

Peter Senge, author of *The Fifth Discipline* (1993) uses the words 'advocacy' and 'inquiry' to describe participation. Talking is principally the means by which we advocate our point of view, our ideas, our thinking. Listening is the process of enquiring into the other person's point of view, their ideas, their thinking.

The best conversations balance advocacy and inquiry. They are a rich mix of talking and listening, of stating views and asking questions.

Three ways to encourage participation

Let's think first about how to encourage others to participate. The important skills here are the skills of enquiry – the skills of good listening. We tend to be very good at talking. We tend not to be so good at listening. And yet it's only by enquiring into the other person's ideas that we can respond well.

The skills of enquiry help us to give other people the respect and space they deserve to develop their own ideas – to make *their* thinking visible. All of these will contribute to more productive and effective meetings.

Paying attention

Attention means concentrating on what the other person is saying. That sounds simple: how can we listen without paying attention?

Of course, we do it most of the time. We think we're listening, but we aren't. We finish the other person's sentences for them. We interrupt. We moan, sigh, grunt, laugh or cough. We fill pauses with our own thoughts, stories or theories. We look at our watches or around the room. We think about the next meeting, or the next report, or the next meal. We frown, tap our fingers, destroy paperclips and glance at our diaries. We give advice. We talk.

A lot of what you hear when someone is speaking to you is *your effect on them*. If you are paying proper attention, they will become more intelligent and articulate. Poor attention will make them hesitate, stumble and doubt the soundness of their thinking. Poor attention makes people more stupid. And that makes the group less intelligent.

Listening well means helping the other person to find out his or her own ideas. The mind containing the problem probably also contains the solution. Their solution is likely to be much better than ours *because it's theirs*. Paying attention means helping the other person to make his or her thinking visible.

Keeping silent

Interrupting is the most obvious symptom of poor attention. It's probably the most common disruptive behaviour in meetings. Mostly we interrupt because we are making assumptions. Here are a few. Next time you interrupt someone in a conversation, ask yourself which assumption you are making:

- My idea is better than theirs.
- The answer is more important than the problem.
- I have to utter my idea and, if I don't interrupt, I'll lose my chance (or forget it).
- I know what they're going to say.
- They don't need to finish the sentence because my rewrite is an improvement.
- They can't improve this idea any further so I might as well improve it for them.
- I'm more important than they are.
- It's more important for me to be seen to have a good idea than for me to let them finish.
- Interrupting will save time.

Interrupting denies the other person respect. It automatically tells them that you don't consider their thinking to be as valuable as yours. It lowers their status. It shatters their confidence that they are able to think for themselves.

Of course, the Chair can improve the quality of the group's conversation immediately by forbidding interruptions. But all the participants must be responsible for their own behaviour. We can all do a little to stop ourselves – and others – from interrupting.

Allowing quiet

Once you stop interrupting, the conversation will become quieter. Pauses will appear. The other person will stop talking – and you won't fill the silence.

Meetings hate pauses. They create discomfort; people begin to feel that we are wasting time. Yet some of the most important thinking in the meeting may happen in the silences between remarks.

These pauses are like junctions. The conversation has come to a crossroads. We have a number of choices about where we might go next. If we are interested in persuading, we will seize the oppor-tunity and make the choice ourselves. But, if we are enquiring, then we give the speaker the privilege of making the choice.

There are two kinds of pause. One is a filled pause; the other is empty. Learn to distinguish between the two. Some pauses are filled with thought. Sometimes, the speaker will stop. The other kind of pause is an empty one. The speaker doesn't stop suddenly; instead, he or she seems to fade away. The energy seems to drop out of the conversation.

Wait out the pause. If the pause is empty, the speaker will probably say so in a few moments. 'I can't think of anything else.' 'That's it, really.' 'So. There we are. I'm stuck now.' Try asking that question: 'Can you think of anything else?' Resist the temptation to move the conversation on by asking a more specific question. The moment you do that, you have closed down every other possible journey that you might take together: you are dictating the road to travel. Make sure that you only do so once the other person is ready to let you take the lead.

Showing that you are paying attention

Our face will show the other person whether we are paying attention. In particular, our eyes will speak volumes to him or her about the quality of our listening.

We often don't know what our face is doing when we listen. We may think we're listening but some tick or expression is saying to the other person: 'I'm bored', or 'I feel threatened by what you're saying', or 'Someone much more interesting has just walked into the room.'

By behaving *as if* you are interested, you can sometimes *become* more interested. Discipline yourself to use an expression that tells the other person that he or she matters to you, that you are interested in what he or she is saying and that you are not in a rush. Try not to frown or tighten your facial muscles. Remember, too, that a rigid smile can be just as off-putting as a perpetual scowl. In the end, your face won't look interested unless you *are* interested.

Treating the speaker as an equal

You will only be able to participate well if you treat others as equals. The moment you make your relationship unequal, the quality of their thinking will suffer.

If you place yourself higher than them in status, you will discourage them from thinking well. If you place them higher than you, you will start to allow your own inhibitions to disrupt your attention to what they are saying.

Patronising the speaker is the greatest enemy of equality in conversations. This conversational sin derives from the way we are treated as children – and the way some of us subsequently treat children. Sometimes we have to treat children like children. We have to decide for them or tell them what they are thinking. We tend to carry this patronising behaviour over into our conversations with adults. It can be subtle: patronising behaviour often covers itself in the guise of being caring or supportive. But it stops people thinking for themselves. It makes them less intelligent. You can't patronise somebody and pay them close attention at the same time.

Cultivating ease

Good thinking happens in a relaxed environment. Cultivating ease will allow the group to enquire more deeply, and discover more ideas.

There's never enough time to do everything we want in a meeting. Busyness tends to foster a culture of urgency. We're so used to urgency that we can't imagine working in any other way. If you're not working flat out, chased by deadlines and juggling 50 assignments at the same time, you're not worth your salary. We cultivate urgency. We assume that the best thinking happens in meetings dominated by urgency.

We're wrong. Urgency keeps people from thinking well. Sometimes, the best results only appear by relaxing: by paying attention to someone else's ideas with a mind that is alert, comfortable and at ease. When we are at ease, the solution to a problem will sometimes appear as if by magic. The swirl of distractions settles into a clear, comfortable sea of thoughts from which ideas emerge like dolphins coming up for air.

Cultivate ease. Slow down. Focus on what needs to be done; put to one side anything that distracts from the job. It's the quality of the decision that matters, not how quickly you reach it. A poor decision made fast will cause more damage than no decision at all.

Stating your case

The ability to persuade and influence has never been in more demand. The days of simply telling people what to do and expecting them to do it are long gone. Now we must all be able to 'sell our ideas'. The progress of our careers may depend on how well we can speak at meetings. Making our point is our opportunity to make our mark and to contribute positively. It's our chance to be noticed.

Applying some very simple principles will make an immediate difference. Nerves can often take over just at the moment we open our mouths. They will show in our shallow breathing, a thin voice, hurried and stuttering words. Here are a few actions that will make a real difference:

- *Make the pace in your speaking.* If the meeting is rushing, slow down. If the conversation is flagging, inject energy. Take the lead.
- *Modulate your voice.* Listen to the music of your voice and try to make it more interesting. Emphasise your points just a little more. Make sure you are speaking loudly enough. Lower the tone of the voice so that you don't sound shrill. Breathe deeply so that your voice gains body.
- *Express yourself accurately.* Beware the temptation to generalise to make your case more convincing. Words like 'always', 'never' or 'everybody' will invite others to pick holes in your argument. On the other hand, try not to contradict yourself! Phrases like 'although, of course', 'well, at the same time' – and 'on the other hand' may confuse your listeners rather than enlighten them. Be specific. Don't deliver too much evidence at once.
- *Look at the group.* Look, in particular, at their eyes (even if they aren't looking at you). Don't look at your notes, at the table, at the floor or at the ceiling. Don't favour any one person. Include everyone in your gaze.
- *Keep calm.* If necessary, hold something to keep your hands still – but don't fiddle with it.
- *Be fearless.* If you know your point is valid, have the courage to support it. If you are genuinely uncertain, say so clearly.

The key to effective persuasion is having powerful ideas and delivering them well. Ideas are the currency of communication.

Information alone will never influence anyone to act. Only ideas have the power to persuade. To persuade, we need to assemble powerful ideas and present them well.

The old word for this skill is 'rhetoric'. Since ancient times, the art of rhetoric has taught how to assemble and deliver ideas. Few of us – at least in Europe – now study rhetoric systematically. Yet, with a few simple principles drawn from this ancient body of knowledge, we can radically improve the quality of our persuasion.

Logos, ethos, pathos

Aristotle, the grandfather of rhetoric, claimed that we can persuade in two ways: through the evidence that we can bring to support our case, and through what he called 'artistic' persuasion.

Evidence might consist of documents or witnesses: we might use spreadsheets and expertise as evidence to support a case. 'Artistic' persuasion combines three internal traits in you as the persuader:

- your character or reputation;
- the quality of your logic;
- the passion that you bring to your argument.

You might say that effective persuasion means communicating equally with your heart, your head and your soul.

Character

Character (or *ethos*) is shorthand for the integrity and authority that you transmit to your audience. Why should your listeners believe what you are telling them? What are your qualifications for saying all this? Where is your experience and expertise? How does your reputation stand with them? What value can you add to the argument from your own experience? Your character creates the trust upon which you can build your argument.

Logic

Logic is the work of rational thought. Reasoning is the method by which you assemble your ideas (the Greeks called it *logos*). Logic comes in two forms.

The first is *deductive logic*, which assembles ideas in a sequence. It begins with an idea, adds a second idea that comments on the first, and draws a conclusion that is the third idea. Here is a classic example of deductive logic:

> Socrates is a man. All men are mortal. Therefore, Socrates is mortal.

A more commercial example might be:

> We are looking to invest in companies with high rates of growth. Company A has a high rate of growth. Therefore, we should invest in Company A.

Inductive logic assembles ideas in a pyramid. It groups ideas together and then summarises them with a governing idea. A simple example might be:

> I've have found three companies that meet our criteria for investment:
>
> 1. Company A meets the criteria.
> 2. Company B meets the criteria.
> 3. Company C meets the criteria.

Passion

Passion (or *pathos*) is the commitment and conviction that you bring to your idea. If you aren't fired up by the idea, you can't expect others to be. To show passion may not be 'the done thing' in your organisation. Yet the great inventors, artists and entrepreneurs are distinguished, not merely by their talent, but by the burning conviction that drove them to achieve, often against great odds.

You can't fake passion. If you want to persuade someone of the power of an idea, you must feel that power in your soul. This may not be easy. After all, not every idea is worth a great deal of passion. But if you want to do a good job, if you want to make your contribution, if you care about the future of your organisation, then passion is probably not far away.

What's the big idea?

If you want to persuade someone, you must have a message.

What do you want to say? What's the big idea? You must know what idea you want to promote. A single governing idea is more likely to persuade your listener than a group of ideas, simply because one strong idea is easier to remember. We work in a world of too much information and too few ideas. Without a driving idea, you will never be able to persuade anyone to believe or do anything.

Working out a message

You may have to think about this before the meeting – or even during the meeting. Ask yourself:

- 'What is my objective?' What do I want to achieve? What would I like to see happen?
- 'Who am I talking to?' Why am I talking about this objective? What does the group already know? What more do they need to know? What do I want them to do? What kind of ideas will be most likely to convince them?
- 'What is the most important thing I have to say to them?' If I am only allowed a few seconds (and you

may only be allowed a brief time) what would I say to convince them?

Try to create a single sentence in your head. Remember that you can't express an idea without uttering a sentence. Does this sentence express what you want to achieve? Is it in language that the listener will understand easily? Is it simple enough? This is a problem particularly when technical specialists try to persuade more senior managers in meetings. The jargon and detail get in the way of the key message that the persuading manager needs to put across.

Taking the meeting with you

Now work out how to bring your listeners to the place where they will accept this message. You must 'bring them around to your way of thinking'. This means starting where the listeners are and gently guiding them to where you want them to be. Once you are standing in the same place, there is a much stronger chance that you will see things the same way. Persuading them will become a great deal easier.

People will only be persuaded by ideas that interest them. Your listeners will only be interested in ideas that address some need or question in their mind. You may be able to state that need, or you may have to *create* a need in their minds.

Here is a simple four-point structure that will help you guide your listeners' thinking. I remember it using the letters SPQR, which you may know as an abbreviation of a Latin motto (*Senatus Populusque Romanus* – 'the senate and people of Rome'). Whether you know the Roman connection or not, these letters seem to be a good way of remembering the sequence.

Situation

Briefly tell the listener what they already know. This demonstrates that you are 'on their wavelength': you understand their situation and can appreciate their point of view. Try to state the situation in such a way that the listener expects to hear more. Think of this as a kind of 'once upon a time...'. It's an opener, a scene-setting statement that prepares them for what's to come. Try using phrases like: 'We all know that...', 'I think we all agree that...', or 'This is the situation.'

Problem

Now identify a problem that has arisen within the situation. The listeners may know about the problem; they may not. But they certainly *should* know about! In other words, the problem should be *their* problem at least as much as yours.

Problems, of course, come in many shapes and sizes. It's important that you identify a problem that the listener will recognise. It must clearly relate to the situation that you have set up: it poses a threat to it or creates a challenge within it. For example:

- Situation: stable, agreed status quo
- Problem
  - something's gone wrong;
  - something could go wrong;
  - something's changed;
  - something could change;
  - something new has arisen;
  - someone has a different point of view;
  - we don't know what to do;
  - there are a number of things we could do.

Problems can be positive as well as negative. You may want to alert your listener to an opportunity that has arisen within the situation.

Question

The problem causes the listeners to ask a question (or would do so, if they were aware of it). Once again, the listeners may or may not be asking the question. If they are, you are better placed to be able to answer it. If they are not, you may have to carefully get them to agree that this question is worth asking.

What's the question?

Situation	**Problem**	**Question**
Stable, agreed status quo	Something's gone wrong	What do we do?
	Something could go wrong	How do we stop it?
	Something's changed	How do we adjust?
	Something could change	How do we prepare?
	Something new has arisen	What could we do?
	Someone has a different point of view	Who's right?
	We don't know what to do	What do we do? *Or* How do we choose?
	There are a number of things we could do	Which course do we take?

Response

Your response or answer to that question is your message. In other words, the message should naturally emerge as the logical and powerful answer to the question raised in the listener's mind by the problem!

This is a classic storytelling framework. It is also well known as a method management consultants use in the introductions to their proposals. Your aim in using it is to guide the listeners from where they are to where you want them to be: to prepare them for your message and the ideas that support it.

The trick is to take your listeners through the four stages *quickly*. Many speakers intuitively use this structure but get bogged down in telling the story; their listeners soon start wishing they would get to the point. Don't be tempted to fill out the story with lots of detail. As you use SPQR, remember these three key points:

1. SPQR should remind the listener rather than persuade them. Until you get to the message, you shouldn't include any idea that you would need to prove.
2. Think of SPQR as a story. Keep it moving. Keep the listener's interest.
3. Adapt the stages of the story to the needs of the listeners. Make sure that they agree to the first three stages without difficulty. Make sure that you are addressing their needs, values and priorities. Put everything in their terms.

Choosing when to speak

Deciding when to speak is almost as important as deciding what to say.

If you speak at the start of the conversation, you may be able to set the tone and the parameters of the discussion. You can take control immediately. Of course, you may then lose it.

In the middle of a conversation, a previous remark may trigger yours or establish the foundation for the point you want to make. Perhaps it contradicts yours, allowing you to make the most of the contrast. Perhaps it was poorly expressed, incomplete, irrelevant or over-emotional. This is your chance to bring the conversation back on track and make others feel more comfortable.

The end of the conversation may be the strongest point of all to make your case. By waiting patiently for everyone else to have their say – and perhaps tie themselves in knots – you have more time to prepare your message. Now you can impress the meeting with a flash of clear thinking. This could give you maximum control over the final decision. It is a high-risk strategy – after all, you may be misjudging whether the conversation is actually ending – but it can be very effective.

8

Problem solving in meetings

Virtually every managerial meeting will involve problem solving of some kind. Problem-solving skills enable us to get what we want: they are the key to success in any organisation and are among the most important skills any manager or team can develop.

Management is solving problems, yet our problem-solving skills are often undeveloped. In particular, teams and other groups who meet to solve problems are rarely trained in the techniques they need. Like parenting, another fundamentally important social skill, problem solving is something we tend to learn piecemeal, by trial and error.

Thinking about problems

Tudor Rickards, in his book *Creativity and Problem Solving at Work* (1990), proposes a set of five problem types:

1. *One-right-answer problems.* We tend to assume that a problem – almost by definition – must have a solution.

In fact, one-right-answer problems are very rare. They must be closely defined and unchanging over time; most practical problems at work are poorly defined and change their shape continually.

2. *Insight problems.* The answers to insight problems surprise us. We discover them, rather than working them out. The discovery is an 'aha' moment. The solution to an insight problem may be logical with hindsight; but we did not arrive at it logically.
3. *Wicked problems.* The solution to a wicked problem cannot be validated until we try it out ('I think this raft will bear our weight: shall we go?'). Many problems are of this kind: solving them may be less difficult than implementing the solution, which requires courage and the ability to anticipate the unexpected.
4. *Vicious problems.* Vicious problems generate solutions that pose even greater problems. Solving the problem of high ground rents by relocating on a remote Scottish island may create huge personnel problems.
5. *Fuzzy problems.* Fuzzy problems have unclear boundaries, making them difficult to solve analytically. Wicked and vicious problems are usually fuzzy, as are 'people problems' and indeed most everyday problems.

We should distinguish between problem solving and decision making. They are closely linked but involve very different kinds of thinking. Deciding is *committing to a course of action*: choosing from among a number of alternatives and making a rational and emotional commitment to that choice. Solving a problem, in itself, may not lead us to do anything; a decision will always result in action of some kind.

Who owns the problem?

Problems in organisations are unlike the theoretical problems we encounter at school or college, primarily because they are 'owned' by real people. Some problems solve themselves, but most problems without owners tend to remain problems without solutions.

First of all, then: identify the problem owner. He or she will become the task leader for the problem-solving session:

- Who is the person most motivated to solve the problem?
- Does he or she want to do something about it?
- Is he or she empowered to act? What sort of action can he or she take? What resources does he or she have available?
- Does the problem owner already have a solution? Is it a good one? Does he or she want to find a new solution, or use the meeting to ratify the current one?
- How committed is the problem owner to finding a solution? Is he or she using the meeting as an exercise to prove that no solution exists?

The problem owner can begin the problem-solving process by presenting the problem to the group. They can explain how it arose, how it affects him or her and the kind of solution he or she is seeking. The group can then respond by categorising the problem, applying the techniques appropriate to the kind of problem under consideration, and developing a solution.

Categorising problems

Different kinds of problem will require different approaches. How we choose to tackle a problem depends on how we choose to look at it. We can categorise problems broadly in two ways: as *presented* problems and *constructed* problems, by examining the structures of problems.

Presented problems are those that happen to us. We have had no control over them, and are not responsible for them. Presented problems prevent us getting where we want to go: they are obstacles in our path. Examples would include:

- the photocopier breaking down;
- a competitor's new product invading our market;
- being stuck in a traffic jam;
- a sudden shift in interest rates.

The defining feature of a presented problem is a discernible gap between what is and what should be. Presented problems create stress. It is like the stress between two jammed machine parts, which threatens to cause damage. It is unwelcome and unpleasant; it causes fatigue. It can be relieved in only two ways: by applying pressure; or by separation. We can seek to overcome the problem, or avoid it: fight or flight.

Constructed problems, by contrast, are challenges that we set ourselves. A constructed problem doesn't exist until we create it. There may not be anything specifically wrong; we are interested in *possibilities*: of improvement, or change, or something different. Examples would include:

- gaining a qualification;
- improving our performance;
- Innovating a new product;
- increasing market share;
- working out a long-term strategy.

The defining feature of a constructed problem is the created gap between what is and what could be. Constructed problems create tension. It is like the tension in a taut rubber band, stretched between current reality and our vision of the future. It is potential energy: it is exciting and energising, and provokes movement.

We can further categorise problems in terms of their structure: *as well structured* or *ill structured*. We can evaluate a problem's structure in terms of its:

- initial conditions (where we are);
- goal conditions (where we want to be);
- operators (the means or methods of moving from initial to goal conditions).

A well-structured problem (WSP) has clear initial conditions, goal conditions and operators. An ill-structured problem (ISP) is unclear in any or all of these respects.

Completing a jigsaw puzzle is a good example of a WSP. *Initial conditions* are clear: the pieces are jumbled together in the box. *Goal conditions* are clear: the finished picture is displayed on the box, and we will know precisely when the solution is complete. *Operators* are clear: categorise pieces by colour, separate all the straight edges, find the corners, compare pieces against the finished picture, and so on. The problem can become more ill-structured in a number of ways: if pieces are missing (initial conditions unclear); if we have no picture on the box (goal conditions unclear); if there are no straight edges, or if all the pieces are of the same colour (operators unclear).

We can now create four categories of problem.

1. Puzzles (presented; WSP)

These are problems according to Kepner and Tregoe's (1976) classic definition: a deviation from the norm. We might call them one-right-answer problems. The archetypal examples are technical: a fault in a machine, an interruption in the power supply, a piece of equipment that won't work properly. The classic problem-solving process – diagnose the cause of the problem, remove the cause, solve the problem – will only work for this type of problem.

2. Headaches (presented; ISP)

These, too, are deviations from the norm; but there is no single or obvious right answer. The problem may have no identifiable cause, or have many causes. Trying to solve a technical problem with no technical expertise is an example of a headache. Much traditional problem solving spends a lot of time and effort trying to turn type 2 problems into type 1 problems. Unfortunately, type 2 problems often have a habit of reverting to type.

3. Planning problems (constructed; WSP)

These are challenges that we set ourselves. We map them out in terms of *objectives*, *targets*, *milestones* and *measures of success*. Examples include working out objectives after an appraisal, setting a budget, giving the team a sales or quality target, or organising a project.

4. Creative problems (constructed; ISP)

These are 'fuzzy' problems. The objective is to find something new: a product or service, a new process, a new territory, a new set of goals. 'People problems' are often of this kind: how to manage or improve a tricky relationship, for example. We are uncertain of the current situation; we may have no precise idea of where we want to go, or how we will know that the problem has been solved. We may not know that we have succeeded until we've tried something (this would be a 'wicked problem'). Tackling such problems demands as open an approach as possible, and takes us into the realms of lateral thinking and brainstorming, where we try to step outside the boundaries of our usual thinking. A task leader in a meeting inviting a creative approach might begin by using statements like:

- 'What I'd really like to do is...'.
- 'If I could break all the rules of reality, I would...'.
- 'This problem is like...'.

There is an important lesson to be learnt from categorising problems in this way. *The only difference between these four types of problem is our perception of them.* We choose to see a problem as being of a certain type. How we go about solving it will depend entirely on that choice. The problem may have moved into another quadrant as we explored it. A puzzle, for example, the more we examine it, may very well become a headache! What seems initially to be a creative problem can become a puzzle or a plan. We can also choose to transform a problem by deliberately moving it into a new quadrant.

The dynamics of problem solving

We tend to have few mental disciplines for solving problems. Most of the logical processes we learn at school only work for one-right-answer problems: mathematical problems or scientific experiments (though experiments, of course, can have unexpected outcomes). In meetings, we are constantly encountering problems that are more complicated and more ambiguous than the neat problems we are set in the classroom – all the more reason to find a systematic approach that will help us to tackle them.

Structuring the process

The process of solving the problem must be structured. Everybody in the group must know what the structure is, what tools and techniques they are expected to use and what behaviours are allowable or inappropriate at each stage. Whatever the problem, it is useful to keep the thinking structure as simple as possible:

1. Identify the problem.
2. Think about the problem.
3. Develop a solution.

The group must be *directed* through this process. Somebody must keep order, preventing the group from jumping forwards or back between stages, urging them to stay with a technique or try something different, controlling the traffic of ideas and behaviour. Responsibility for this facilitative task best rests with a process director, who should be somebody other than the problem owner – probably the Chair. Other participants in the meeting become resources at the service of the problem owner, led in their thinking by the Chair or process director.

An easy way to envisage this is to imagine the group as an 'ideas consultancy'. The Chair is the lead consultant, and the problem owner is the 'client'. The group should treat the problem owner with the same respect they would give any client: listening carefully to their concerns, tailoring their thinking to the specific issues the client brings to the meeting, checking their ideas with the client at various stages. The group may sometimes need to separate itself physically from the 'client': particularly in order to generate ideas without the danger of being limited by the 'client's' assumptions or negative responses.

The greatest danger of problem-solving meetings is that the group will leap to a judgement, ignoring first-stage thinking and plunging headlong into the second stage. We may feel a sense of urgency – we need a solution quickly – or believe that if we investigate the problem too much, it will become even more difficult to deal with! Such leaps to judgement tend to cause the problem to return to haunt us. If a problem recurs regularly, it is probably because of 'quick fixes' in the past – solutions applied too hastily and insufficiently thought through.

Good problem solving relies on good first-stage thinking. This applies in all three steps of the process: evidence, interpretation, action. Do not be afraid to spend more time in first-stage thinking, exploring issues, adding information or reconstructing the problem. Such time will rarely be wasted.

Stage 1: identify the problem

If we are working out ways to get from where we are to where we want to be, we need first to investigate where we are as *fully as possible*. We must ask three questions:

- What is the current situation?
- Does a gap exist between this situation and a more desirable one?
- Are we certain that we do not already have a satisfactory means of closing the gap?

Obvious as they sound, many problem-solving groups fail to ask these questions. As a result, they waste a great deal of time trying to solve several different problems at once, or irrelevant problems, or problems that do not exist.

Ask the problem owner to present the problem to the meeting. Listen carefully to what he or she says and ask questions to improve the group's understanding of the issue. *Avoid suggesting solutions*. Group members will probably begin to think in terms of solutions very quickly: encourage them to note them down privately for consideration later. If somebody does suggest a solution openly, 'park' it on a sheet of flipchart paper and move on.

Stage 2: think about the problem

Having identified the problem, and the category it best fits, we can begin to apply the tools and techniques appropriate to the task.

Puzzles

A puzzle is a presented problem, and the essence of a presented problem is that it is outside us. We take no responsibility for its existence – only for solving it or finding a way of living with it.

We act on puzzles; we remain fundamentally unaffected by them.

By choosing to look at the problem as a puzzle, we choose to treat it *objectively*: to analyse it rationally, seeking causes or effects or splitting the problem into parts and tackling each part systematically. In order to deal effectively with a puzzle, we must give it as clear a structure as possible.

We tackle puzzles by using heuristics: put simply, methods of finding things out (the word, from the Greek, is related to 'eureka'). A mathematical formula is an example of a well-structured heuristic. Other heuristics may be less exact, but no less useful. Six broad categories are particularly important:

a. *Proximity.* How close are we to the problem? Can we find our way towards the problem by locating it in context or by solving related problems?
b. *One step at a time.* Can we break the problem down into parts and solve each part in order?
c. *Means and ends.* Can we separate our goal from the means of getting there? What is our overall objective? What do we need in order to achieve it?
d. *Modelling.* Can we make a model of the problem? This would simplify it and allow us to manipulate the model to assess possible outcomes.
e. *Analogy.* What is the problem like? Can we find a concrete example of something similar? What are the similarities? What are the differences?
f. *Abstraction.* What is the overall, simple shape of the problem? Can we summarise it? Does the summary suggest a simple solution? Could we then apply means-and-ends analysis to work out how to achieve it?

Headaches

Headaches, too, are presented problems but, unlike puzzles, we cannot be cool and objective about them. They cause us pain. The pain is a sign that we are no longer outside the problem.

We may not have been responsible for it, but we have become involved: it affects other parts of our work, we feel forced to take responsibility for its consequences. This discrepancy between our involvement and our lack of responsibility is what makes it a headache.

We can deal with a headache in two ways: use a painkiller, or remove the stress that causes it. The equivalent in problem solving to an analgesic is known as the 'quick fix'. It treats the symptoms without tackling the cause of the problem. Repeatedly doing things rather than delegating them is a good example of a quick fix. The quick fix may be attractive because it produces immediate results and can therefore be seen to be 'working'. But because the root cause of the problem remains unsolved, the problem recurs and the quick fix becomes a regular fix. We become dependent and, eventually, addicted.

A more effective approach to a headache is to find a way to remove the stress that causes it. This may involve transforming it into a puzzle, a plan or a creative problem. Perhaps we can make the problem better structured. Or we can move the headache in another direction. We may choose to turn it into a constructed problem. By transforming our perception of the problem, we take responsibility for it: it becomes a challenge that we can feel comfortable accepting, rather than an obstacle that we cannot move.

Planning problems

A planning problem is a constructed problem. The essence of a constructed problem is that we 'own' it. It's not a matter of 'me acting on the problem', but of 'me being with the problem' or rather, of the problem becoming a part of me.

Athletes training for the Olympics are not acting on the problem of how to win: they are living the challenge of improving their performance. Similarly, when we accept the challenge of a constructed problem, we take responsibility for our own performance and for the outcome, whatever it may be.

It is always possible to transform a presented problem into a constructed problem. Such a transformation:

- gives us responsibility for the problem;
- helps to convert stress into tension – into potential energy for change;
- transforms an obstacle into an opportunity;
- widens our choice of action.

The simplest way to create a constructed problem is to cast it as a 'how to' statement. For example:

> How to install a new system throughout the organisation by the end of the year.

This challenge is a planning problem. It is well structured in terms of initial conditions and goal conditions. To be thoroughly well structured, we must clarify our operators: our plan, and the measures of satisfaction by which we can judge our success in completing it.

Planning meetings are one of the most common in management. They may be relatively straightforward or horribly complicated – depending on the number of activities to be coordinated. Leaping to judgement is as much a risk in solving a planning problem as with any other. It's easy to get lost in the complexity of detail and lose sight of your overall objective. First-stage thinking here involves asking: 'What are we trying to achieve?', 'How will we know when we have achieved it?'

Work out your plan *backwards* from your objective, rather than forwards from where you are.

Creative problems

Creative problems are fuzzy constructed problems. The less well defined a problem is, the more amenable it is to creative treatment. We will probably never find ourselves tackling a problem creatively by accident. We must *deliberately choose* the creative approach. We would make that choice where:

- we can find no single identifiable cause;
- we cannot remove the cause or causes;
- we have too little (or too much) information about the problem;
- the information is ambiguous;
- we have no precedent to follow;
- the variables are difficult to measure;
- time is limited;
- we want to do something different.

A little thought will suggest that some of these factors characterise a good many of the problems we face in our organisations. Creative thinking is not a desirable extra that we might consider bolting on to our existing managerial skills. It is, increasingly, a critical ability that we must all foster.

Deciding to take a creative approach may not be easy. We are straying into unfamiliar territory; we may find nothing, or something with implications far beyond the original problem. We must weigh up, therefore, the possible consequences of *not* 'going creative' on a problem. Suppose we are missing something of enormous benefit by not exploring? Suppose a competitor finds it and puts us out of business?

At the heart of creative problem solving is an *excursion*. We are taking a journey away from the original problem, to find something somewhere else that we can bring back as a potentially useful solution.

The first step is to ask the problem owner to cast the problem as a 'how to' statement. For example, 'a piece of machinery breaking down' can become 'how to repair the machinery'. The group can then create new 'how to' statements:

- how to repair the machinery:
  - how to stop the machinery breaking down;
  - how to achieve targets without using the machinery;
  - how to manage with faulty machinery;
  - how to build our machinery maintenance skills.

It is this *range* of 'how to' statements that is important. They create possibilities by enriching our perception of the problem. An effective 'how to' session might generate 50 to 100 new statements from a single idea.

Any meeting that is stuck on a problem can find new ideas by conducting a 'how to' session. The technique helps us to look for goals rather than obstacles, at the future instead of the past. We can enrich this process by using backward planning. By regarding the initial 'how to' as a solution rather than a problem, we move backwards, asking what higher-level problem it might solve. We can repeat the process with the new problem, and so on. Higher-level 'how to' statements will be more general than the original; we might then think forwards from these general ideas towards other specific 'how to' statements that we have not so far found.

The problem owner, faced with an array of 'how to' statements, might then sort them and decide which to pursue. Three classes might emerge:

- *realistic courses of action* – that we might consider applying immediately or putting to one side as fallback solutions;
- *embryonic ideas* – needing development to become feasible;
- *implausible ideas* – vague, nonsensical or seemingly impossible.

The implausible ideas are those with the greatest creative potential. If you want to pursue a creative approach, pick the most implausible idea and work on it. If the idea also has a 'wow' dimension – if the problem owner feels excited by the idea in some way – so much the better.

Stage 3: develop the solution

Whatever the problem we have tackled, we must evaluate any solution we find and develop it as a feasible proposition in the real world. Once the group has presented its solutions to the problem owner and he or she has chosen the solution that he or she finds most attractive, the problem owner should paraphrase it back to the meeting to demonstrate that he or she understands it. The group as a whole can then evaluate the solution to identify its strengths and potential weaknesses.

Evaluating the solution

The easiest way to do this is to examine the positive, negative and interesting aspects of our solution, in order. The discipline of attending to each set of features in turn will help us to think about them more objectively.

Looking for what is good about a solution will strengthen it. The positive features of any idea will give it added credibility when it comes to be presented to others (who may be all too ready to criticise or reject it). Looking for its weak features will give us the opportunity to work on them, develop or eliminate them before they see the light of day. By assessing what is interesting about an idea, we begin to reveal its potential impact, and can begin to think about the challenges of implementing it:

- Identify *positive* aspects of the idea: whatever makes it attractive. Do not worry if you cannot think of many. Persist: think only about positive features. For each one, ask: 'What further benefits would that bring?' For every benefit, ask: 'How else could we achieve them?' Yet more new ideas may suddenly begin to emerge.

- Now list the aspects that are *negative* or problematic: weaknesses, shortcomings, risks and dangers. For each one, ask: 'So what is it I need to find?' and try to answer with a 'how to' statement. In this way, a single presented problem can easily turn into six or more potential ways of improving the idea.
- Finally, list the *interesting* aspects of the idea: implications arising from it, the consequences of implementing it, how it will affect other people, potential by-products or spin-offs.

How/how analysis

To strengthen an idea into a workable proposal, we must identify the steps to implement it. Begin with the solution and ask 'How do we do that?' Identify a small number of actions. For each of them, ask in turn how they can be achieved. After three or four stages, a number of possible 'chains' of action have been worked out, from broad idea through to specific detail.

A 'how/how' analysis allows us to:

- see alternative courses of action clearly;
- sift feasible courses of action from implausible ones;
- identify recurring actions, or detailed actions that will accomplish more than one step;
- work out a plan of action.

At the final step in the problem-solving process, we are working out the next steps. What began as a meeting to solve a problem has become a meeting to decide on action. If we fail to work out what to do, all our problem solving will have been a waste of time.

9

After the meeting

No meeting is ever an end in itself. Meetings form part of an ongoing cycle in the lives of managers and organisations. Meetings result in actions, which provoke change, which itself must be evaluated, calling for new meetings.

Everybody has responsibilities after the meeting. The Chair, administrator and participants all have duties to fulfil. If we fail in our responsibilities after the meeting, all the effort that has gone into making the meeting effective and efficient will have been wasted.

The chair: following up actions

Meetings are judged by their results. The Chair is responsible for ensuring that the actions agreed during the meeting are completed.

Delegate as many actions as possible. This will:

- relieve you of some of the burden;
- give ownership of actions to participants;
- demonstrate trust; and
- build the team.

All agreed actions should have a named 'Actioner'. Actioners should feel that they 'own' the action: they should understand why they are doing it and have the authority – and resources – to carry it through. The Chair must ensure that nobody takes on an unrealistic amount of work.

Schedule actions to happen as soon as possible. Prompt action is more likely to be taken by participants fired with enthusiasm by the meeting they have just left.

All actions should be agreed in the knowledge of:

- the meeting's and individual's authority to act;
- the implications for other staff, departments, or organisations;
- the probable costs;
- the resources available.

Back up all decisions and actions in writing.

A summary action sheet distributed with or before the full minutes can be useful. Others affected by the action may need to be contacted by memo or e-mail.

You will want to follow up actions at an appropriate time. Don't let follow-up disappear amid all the other fires you have to fight; but take care not to pester, particularly if participants have volunteered.

Don't simply reschedule uncompleted actions. Discuss the reasons for failure: is the delegated person overloaded? Perhaps the action was unrealistic or circumstances suddenly changed.

The Chair has one other main responsibility: overseeing the production of the minutes. This may be a delicate task. You may be tempted to amend the administrator's first draft: perhaps for diplomatic reasons; sometimes, more sinisterly, for political ones. Minutes that are 'economical with the truth' are unprofessional and unethical. More often the problem falls into a grey area where sensibilities must be tactfully respected while accuracy is maintained.

The administrator: writing the minutes

Few of us want to read lengthy minutes. Their very name suggests something brief ('minute' as in 'tiny'). Minutes are a *brief* summary of events. They are not a word-by-word description of all that is said in a meeting. The term 'verbatim minutes' is a contradiction in terms. Minutes are a record of facts, decisions and agreed actions. Your aim must be to keep the minutes as brief as possible.

Make sure that you are clear from the outset what is required. Check with the Chair on matters of layout and style.

Write up the minutes as soon as possible after the meeting: within 24 hours if you can. They should follow the agenda exactly, with identical numbers and item headings. They might include:

- the name of the meeting;
- the venue, date and time;
- the names of the Chair, administrator and participants;
- apologies for absence;
- previous minutes agreed and signed;
- matters arising;
- summaries of each item;
- summaries of submitted reports;
- motions and amendments;
- proposer's and seconder's names for each motion or amendment;
- voting numbers;
- decisions reached;
- actions agreed, with names and deadlines;
- venue, date, and time of next meeting;
- date of completion and at least one signature, usually the Chair's. The administrator's signature is a welcome addition.

Lay out the minutes as attractively as possible. Allow a wide left margin and plenty of space between items. Highlight actions to be taken, perhaps using bold type, underlining, by placing them in a column on the right-hand side, or by listing them on a separate sheet.

Constructing a minute

The most effective minutes are carefully planned and laid out. Think of constructing your minutes, rather than simply writing them.

Background

You must put the item in context for readers who were not at the meeting. The item title may do the job; if not, indicate briefly how the matter arose.

Discussion

How much to include? There is no need to attribute statements to particular individuals unless they ask you to do so. You should take care to include references to:

- recent events;
- dates and place names;
- names of people met or interviewed;
- sums of money;
- legal necessities;
- agreements or contracts;
- policies;
- documentation (reports, correspondence);
- names of departments or other organisations.

Decision

A summary of what has been agreed. There is no need to add lengthy reasons or justification for the decision. Summarise the reasons for the decision as briefly as possible.

Action

What is to be done: by whom, when and where. Actions should be highlighted.

Yours will be the definitive record of the meeting. The minutes must satisfy everybody who attended, and this may require a certain amount of tact. Concentrate on facts, decisions and actions, and you will be less likely to go wrong.

Allow yourself time to check the minutes before presenting them to the Chair and distributing them. Check paragraphs, sentence length, unnecessary dialogue, passive verbs and the use of tense.

Paragraphs and sentences

The style of minutes varies enormously between organisations. Some documents will look like lengthy papers; other minutes – particularly in more high-tech companies – will be spreadsheets, with text reduced to an absolute minimum. The key to effective minute-writing is to be able to improve the quality of the document within the parameters set by your manager, by legal requirements and by the traditions of your organisation.

For my money, minutes should mostly be written in full sentences. Sentences allow you to express your meaning with maximum clarity. Anything more abbreviated risks creating ambiguity and uncertainty in the reader's mind. And sentences may well be grouped into short paragraphs.

Paragraphs

Each major contribution to the item will have a separate paragraph. Use sub-paragraphs for substantial amounts of important detail, or lists of points. As a rough guideline, try not to extend any block of text to more than four lines.

Sentence length

No sentence should be longer than 25 words. A sentence will

probably be too long if it contains too many ideas. Begin by identifying its main idea. Remove everything else: other ideas can be expressed in their own sentences or, if they are less important, can be consigned to oblivion. Remember: the more important the idea, the more briefly it should be expressed.

Stylistic traps to avoid

There are a number of specific pitfalls that minute-writers can fall into. Avoid them, and you will help your reader to make more sense of your work.

Unnecessary dialogue

Avoid the 'He said, she said' syndrome! Weed out verbs like: reported, discussed, explained, proposed, expressed concern, suggested, confirmed, requested, asked, introduced, and so on:

> Mr Brown reported that he had spoken to the importers on Thursday...
> Brian and Mary discussed the downturn in sales figures...
> Geraldine suggested that the options seemed clear. Derek disagreed...
> Sola expressed concern to Fiona that her team was underperforming.
> Fiona told Sola...

Have you inadvertently slipped into recording what was said, rather than facts or thoughts? What can you remove? What could you put differently or more briefly?

> Mr Brown spoke to the importers on Thursday... Sales figures fell....
> The options for action became clear. Fiona's team is not underperforming.

Passive verbs

Passive verbs are the curse of minutes everywhere! Of course minutes must be unbiased, but this does not mean that every verb should be passive:

Many points of view were expressed... It was agreed that...
It was thought necessary to...
The resolution however was not passed...
The plans were considered at considerable length...

Passive verbs describe actions that the subject of the sentence suffers or undergoes. They always consist of a part of the verb 'to be' and a past participle. The 'grammar check' on your computer will almost certainly be programmed to seek out passive verbs – though it may not be very effective at finding all of them. You can use your grammar check facility to help you recognise passives more easily. Wherever possible, substitute active verbs, which cut down the length of sentences and accurately allocate responsibility:

Everybody expressed his or her point of view...
The committee agreed that...
We must...
The resolution failed.
The meeting considered the plans at length...

Tense

This is another bone of contention. 'Minutes should be written throughout in the past tense', say some authorities. Why? Certainly statements of what took place during the meeting are best expressed in the past tense:

Tom presented a report on current car fleet usage.

Don't feel, however, that you must rigorously avoid the use of the present tense. The result will be unnatural, cumbersome and almost unreadable:

Tom presented a report on current car fleet usage. He revealed that some sales staff had been claiming for unreasonably high mileage figures. After considerable discussion, it was agreed that Tom would continue to monitor expense forms and would report back to the team at the next meeting.

The minutes, after all, are dated: there is no reason why statements of current information should not be put in the present tense:

> Some sales staff are still claiming for unreasonably high mileages.

Use the future for actions to be taken:

> Tom will continue to monitor expense forms and report back at the next meeting.

The resulting minute is still accurate: it is now also much easier to read.

Provided that meaning is not sacrificed, abbreviated notes can be just as effective for action statements:

> Tom reported on current car fleet usage. Some sales staff still making unreasonable mileage claims. ACTION: Tom to continue to monitor expense forms, and to report back at next team meeting.

Ambiguous wording

Points made clearly in the meeting may become dangerously ambiguous when condensed into a minute. Watch for the following.

Vagueness

Most departments are still failing to supply figures... (Which departments exactly?)
Several managers have commented adversely on the new system... (Who are they?)
Some of the machines are still failing regularly. (How many?)
Staff elsewhere have been notably successful... (Where?)
Problems recently/in the near future/at some point... (When?)

Euphemism

Delays in delivery are causing some concern. (How much concern? Is the matter urgent?)
Management is not entirely happy with the new arrangement. (Are they a bit happy? Or actually angry?)

Ambiguous word order

Jeff reported on redirecting sewage to the Works Committee.
After releasing toxic gases into the atmosphere, Bernard reported that his equipment was now in good repair.

Participating after the meeting

Do you feel that you 'own' the action you have agreed to take? Do you understand why you are doing the job? Are you empowered to do it? You must have the necessary:

- authority;
- instructions;
- resources;
- budget;
- staff;
- information.

You need to:

- Show willing – if you don't, you may get picked on!
- Don't take on too much – you may fail and praise may turn to mockery.
- Act promptly – don't delay. You may forget vital information. Circumstances may change sooner than you think and make the job even more complicated.
- Report back as agreed – either directly to the Chair or at the next meeting.

- Liaise – your actions may well link to those of others who were at the meeting and will probably form the basis for future agenda items.

Finally: do you feel that your contribution is being recognised and appreciated? If not: proclaim your success!

10

Different meetings and how to run them

Most managers find themselves regularly holding meetings of particular kinds. This chapter examines six of the most common and offers you guidance on how to conduct them:

- team meetings;
- negotiations;
- brainstorming sessions;
- mealtime meetings;
- electronic meetings;
- international meetings.

Remember to go into any meeting with a clear sense of your *purpose*. What do you want to achieve? How are you going to manage the meeting to achieve that objective? What kind of conversation do you need to hold?

Team meetings

Teams must meet frequently. The danger for any regular meeting is that it can become routine: soon it comes to be regarded more with dread than interest. The solution might be to change the way the meetings are run. A team leader who is willing to delegate functions will lead team meetings that are more active, more interesting and more successful. Consider holding your next team meeting like this:

- Construct the agenda prior to the meeting. There's no need to be too formal about this. Anyone who wants to contribute sends a note or adds it to the list. E-mail is particularly valuable for this.
- Finalise the agenda at the start of the meeting. Each participant must justify the inclusion of his or her item. The meeting decides whether it is worthy of discussion (perhaps another team member can solve the problem outside the meeting: a brief conversation, a memo, a report put in the internal post).
- Allocate timings to all agenda items. The whole meeting has a maximum length – decided on by you, the team leader – which must not be exceeded. The aim is not to fill the allotted time but to complete the meeting as quickly as possible.
- The agenda is now complete. Nothing else is allowed until the next meeting.
- Each item is 'owned' by the participant who submitted it. As discussion progresses, he or she must ask:
  - is the task or problem clearly understood?
  - is expertise identified?
  - is knowledge shared?
  - am I creating a cooperative climate in the group?
  - is everyone being heard?
  - can a decision be reached by consensus – without a vote?

  - is the Chair's role reduced to a minimum?
- Rotate the Chair's role. The Chair for each item becomes the minute-taker for the next item, recording the minutes on a flipchart for all to see.
- Keep to time rigorously. Clock-watching is the responsibility of the team as a whole.
- Summarise all decisions and actions at the end of the meeting. Invite any initial suggestions for the next meeting.

Most team meetings will cover the 'Four Ps':

- *Progress.* Our achievements. Include individual achievements if appropriate. Reflect back to the team what we have done so far to reach our goals. Start with progress because it helps to create a positive feeling in the team.
- *Policy.* How developments elsewhere in the organisation are affecting what we are doing.
- *People.* Any relevant matters affecting team members that will strengthen the team.
- *Points for action.* What we need to do in the future. Any new targets, or special points for action.

This procedure increases the team's ownership of the meeting. A climate of openness allows all views to be expressed with equal authority; solutions are arrived at by agreement rather than imposed. In one company where team leaders introduced this procedure, teams cut meeting time by a third.

Team briefing

Team briefing develops the team meeting into a management information system. The objective of team briefing is to ensure that every employee knows and understands what he or she and others in the organisation are doing – and why. Team leaders and their teams get together regularly, for about half an hour, to talk about issues relevant to them and their work. The team leader's brief is based on a 'core brief' supplied by senior management but, along with this 'cascade' element of information relayed down the line, each team leader writes his or her own brief.

The advocates of team briefing emphasise that it also allows teams to evaluate the brief, assess its relevance to their own work, and communicate in turn back up the line. There are a number of other benefits to team briefing:

- *It reinforces management.* The briefing meeting is an opportunity for the team leader to lead. This is particularly important for first-line managers, reminding them of their leadership responsibilities and of their accountability for their team's performance. Team briefing gives management credibility, and ensures that the team hears management information from a manager.
- *It increases commitment.* Briefing improves the team's commitment to their objectives, and to those of the organisation. Explaining why a job needs doing is as important as telling people that it has to be done.
- *It prevents misunderstandings.* The 'grapevine' of rumour and speculation is often a threat to team morale and effectiveness. Team briefing helps to keep the vine well pruned!
- *It helps to facilitate change.* To quote Peter Senge (1993): people do not resist change; they resist being changed. Team briefing helps to keep people in touch with what is happening, and to give them the means to contribute to change rather than be victims of it.
- *It improves upward communication.* Asking people for ideas in an information vacuum is like asking them to think without brain cells. People will probably not

> volunteer ideas if they are not asked for them; briefing gives senior management the regular opportunity to make that request. It also provides a permanent channel for feedback and other upward communication.

Team briefing, unlike more informal team meetings, must be led by team leaders. Because the briefer should be the manager accountable for the team's performance, it may make more sense to brief people in teams rather than according to managerial status: line managers with their production line team, for example, rather than with other managers. The choice of briefer can be affected, too, by the size of teams: if teams are too small or too large, communication, control and interaction all suffer.

There is a danger that team briefing can become merely a system of 'top-down' information flow, conducted in a paternalistic, quasi-military manner. It can be easy for senior management to assume that teams only need to know about decisions to commit to them. The success of team briefing depends on fostering genuine dialogue.

Team briefing also relies on systematic implementation to be thoroughly effective. If you are a team leader, you can set briefings yourself; but they will be much more effective if they are part of a wider communication process and structure within your organisation.

Negotiations

Every manager has to be able to negotiate. Doing deals is a fundamental way to achieve goals; but it is a means, not an end. A successful negotiation closes with everybody satisfied; the effective negotiator is delighted when the meeting creates genuine agreement.

The great risk in negotiating is adversarial thinking. The very concept of negotiation implies two sides (or more). As a result, scoring over the opposition becomes the primary strategy. Each side tries to 'get the edge', on the assumption that the other is doing the same. The negotiation becomes a complicated exercise in playing games: secrecy, bullying, hoodwinking – all the familiar symptoms of 'looking out for number one'.

This tacit agreement that negotiation is hostile creates stress, wastes time and generates flawed agreements. As long as this attitude stalks the negotiation, catastrophe will follow, new problems will arise, commitment will suffer, promises will be broken, relationships will deteriorate and reputations will be bruised.

If you are negotiating, your responsibility is to seek agreement: a specific plan of action to which all parties can commit themselves. You will only achieve real commitment on both sides if you pay close attention to the group's social objectives, moving carefully through the four stages of group development.

Stage 1: forming

Relationships at the beginning of a negotiation may, of course, be hostile. The negotiation may be taking place against a background of confrontation, or people may feel that mutual trust risks being damaged. Whatever the background, people will be expecting hostility because that is our usual experience of negotiation. If you want to break through this hostility to real agreement, you must work hard to establish rapport at the very beginning of the meeting. Rapport is not merely a matter of being polite. Hard questions need to be asked:

- Do we want to negotiate?
- What exactly are we negotiating about?
- What are the long-term and short-term objectives, on both sides?

Know exactly what you want. Where is your bottom line? Beware greed or comparison with others: establish what you need, what you can do without, what will make you truly satisfied.

Ask the same questions of the other side. Imagine yourself into their position. What do they want? What do they *really* want? What are their hopes and plans? Who do they represent? What are they looking for now? How important is it to them? Can you see any way of giving them what they want without losing what you want?

Do your homework: numbers, public and private statements, reports, relationships with background interests. Do not be fooled by initial postures, which may be deceptive. Inspect the other side's position and *invite them to inspect your own position.* Admit uncertainty. Expose potential problems on your side. Honesty will boost your credibility and can be surprisingly disarming.

Stage 2: storming

Establish the areas of difference and examine the reasons for them. At this stage, what may seem to be differences of objective may be different versions or perceptions of reality.

Work hard to establish norms: of the task (hard data both sides can agree on, measures of satisfaction – how will we know when we have reached agreement?); and of behaviour (what we find acceptable, what we cannot allow). Demonstrate your honesty.

Be assertive: neither aggressive in defence of your own position nor submissive to every proposition from the other side. Show the other side that you recognise the rules by which you are both playing: question them, if necessary.

Stage 3: norming

Work from agreed norms towards possible solutions or ways forward. Persist and be patient. Expect the conversation to move one step forward and two back – or even sideways. Sideways moves may be clues to new solutions that neither side has thought of yet.

Be on the lookout continually for new ways to view the issue and new ways of handling it. Offer choices and keep options open. Challenge your own assumptions and resist the temptation to reject ideas. Work through 'what if' scenarios and invite the other side to inspect your own thinking. This will only work well if you are truly open to inspection and willing to alter your views.

Identify sticking points. Are they fundamental differences, the results of different perspectives or behavioural posturing (face-saving, demonstrating firmness to vested interests)? When you get truly stuck, go back to first principles. Why are we here? What is our objective?

Stage 4: performing

Recognise when the deal is done. Negotiations often collapse because the negotiators do not notice when they have reached agreement. The adversarial nature of negotiation creates the underlying assumption that agreement is not possible. You may continue to press for advantage after seeming to have won. This is another certain route to breakdown.

Act as if the other side will be your public relations agency. The truth is that they will. What others say about you is how they see you. Your reputation as a negotiator is your most valuable asset in future negotiations. Guard it well.

Brainstorming sessions

Brainstorming is a structured process for having ideas. Unlike problem solving, where the aim is to arrive at a single solution, brainstorming aims to generate as many ideas as possible. Brainstorming is structured first-stage thinking.

It was invented in the 1930s by Alex Osborn, an advertising executive (see Osborn, 1963). It has been developed since by a number of practitioners, including Bill Gordon (1961) and George Prince (1970), the developers of Synectics, and Edward de Bono (1982), whose concept of lateral thinking embodies the very essence of brainstorming: thinking 'sideways' to find a new idea, rather than 'vertically' towards a logical conclusion.

Brainstorming operates according to a few simple principles. They are easy to remember, yet many brainstorming sessions fail to observe them. Alex Osborn's four rules of brainstorming are:

1. *Criticism is ruled out.* Ideas are to be judged later, not during the session.
2. *'Freewheeling' is welcome.* The wilder the idea, the better. It's easier to tame down than to think up.
3. *We want more!* The more ideas, the greater the likelihood of a good new one.
4. *Combine and improve.* As well as contributing ideas, team members should suggest ways of improving, combining, or varying others' ideas.

Beyond these simple rules, Osborn emphasises the importance of:

- getting going – not waiting for inspiration to strike;
- focus – on the objective of the session, what we want to achieve;
- attention – of the whole team to one kind of thinking at a time;

- concentration – sticking at it, refusing to give up if no ideas come.

Brainstorming sessions need to be prepared carefully. The danger is that people will not understand what kind of thinking they should be doing during the session. You might consider some further techniques to make it more interesting.

Setting targets

The discipline of 'scoring' can produce more ideas and help crazier ideas to surface. A target of between 50 and 100 ideas in 10 minutes is not unreasonable for a competent team of about seven people.

Varying the structure

Change the way the session runs by:

- briefing the team with the problem a day beforehand, to allow for private musing and 'sleeping on the problem';
- beginning the session with a warm-up exercise, unrelated to the task in hand;
- taking breaks between techniques, to allow people's minds to relax and discover new ideas.

Separating individual and group brainstorming

An idea is only ever the product of a single mind. Solitary thinking is best for having ideas; group thinking for building on them. Brainstorming can benefit from using both.

Ask people to generate ideas individually to begin the process. Gather them anonymously, to encourage the wilder ideas to surface and counter any politics or inhibitions in the team. Then use group brainstorming to integrate the ideas, build on them, combine them, vary them, develop them and transform them.

Mealtime meetings

Business lunches, and now breakfast meetings, are increasingly popular. My own feeling is that they are of limited value. Eating and meeting simply don't mix very well. The informality of a meal can work against the clarity of thinking necessary in a meeting. Objectives may be unclear because there is no formal agenda. The professional and social aspects of meeting are dangerously mixed. Hidden agendas may be hard at work.

The best advice is probably not to schedule mealtime meetings at all. Separate the two activities – and meet before eating! If you find yourself invited to a mealtime meeting, take a few simple precautions:

- Decide on your own private agenda. Are you going to meet – or eat?
- If the meeting is worth attending, you must be prepared not to eat too much.
- Avoid alcohol.
- Taking notes will be difficult. Arm yourself with a narrow pad that can slip easily between plates and glasses.

Electronic meetings

More and more meetings are being held electronically, either over the telephone or via a video link. Electronic meetings are designed to cut costs, but they obviously rely on all the participants being in place, on time.

Everybody should be aware of a few other key principles to ensure that electronic meetings run smoothly:

- *Allow pauses between speakers.* A single word overlapping another speaker will cause considerable delay while the last remark is repeated. A teleconference has its own, peculiar rhythm, which is easily picked up with a little practice.
- *Use names frequently.* Announce yourself by name, particularly if you haven't spoken for some time. Announce whom you are addressing, and who you would like to speak next.
- *Choose your words with care.* The fact that people are not physically together places great weight on the words used. There is a lot of opportunity for misunderstanding and much may need to be laboriously explained in the absence of a visual component.
- *Avoid hidden agendas.* Teleconferences without video are vulnerable to conspiracies: notes passed silently between participants in one room; gestures and facial expressions mocking the ignorance of those at the other end of the line. Order must be maintained. On the other hand, it can sometimes be easier to be brutally frank when the other person is 500 miles away.
- *On video, ensure that everybody is visible.* Hidden voices and disembodied hands swimming into shot are distracting.

International meetings

We conduct more and more of our business internationally. As organisations operate more globally, and as our own society grows more and more diverse, we find ourselves increasingly meeting with people from different cultures.

Different cultures exist within one country, and within individual organisations. Sensitivity to cultural background is, of course, a basic prerequisite of modern business practice. We can identify two main areas in particular that determine the way we interact in meetings. First, beliefs about the organisation. How do we view 'the way we do things around here'? How do we manage information and communicate with each other? Second, beliefs about leadership. Who has power? How do they wield it? How do we make decisions? How do we think together?

Our behaviour in meetings will also be determined by other factors. You need to consider the values each individual brings into the room: family values, religious or ethical values, considerations of education, etiquette, respect for others, the way work is carried out. And, behind each person stands the history of his or her country, ethnic group or people. It is impossible to ignore the wider tensions (or friendships) that may exist between national or ethnic groups, or the history that may have brought people together.

Each meeting should aim to create common ground between those who attend it. The objectives of the meeting should be realistic and work-oriented, but it is also a chance for people to increase their understanding of each other. The best way to minimise culture clash is to make sure that the purpose of the meeting is made crystal clear, and that procedures within the meeting accommodate everybody's expectations.

Language

The meeting will undoubtedly be held in one language. Anybody not fluent in that language will feel seriously disadvantaged. The choice of language for the meeting can itself be a serious cultural or even political matter. Arrange for papers to be translated if necessary. You may decide that speakers can speak in any language comprehensible to all, or that they should bring personal translators with them.

Preparation

Different business cultures create different expectations of meetings. For some, the most important work is conducted outside the meeting: at dinner the night before, or in the coffee break. Your procedures may need to allow for this, by scheduling social events before or after the meeting.

Distribute papers well in advance with specific requests for comments. This will give you some idea of the nature of participants' preparation.

During the meeting

Don't be alarmed if people seem to behave unusually. What may seem unacceptably rude to you – avoiding eye contact, giving direct answers to questions, leaving the meeting without warning to make a phone call, disregarding formal procedure – may be normal behaviour in another culture.

Agree the agenda before and at the start of the meeting. Pay special attention to the purpose of individual items, which participant will speak on them, and what decisions are expected from each. Announce how you expect people to contribute.

After the meeting

Getting agreement on decisions or actions is notoriously problematic in cross-cultural meetings. Are people agreeing to act, or being polite? What is being agreed to? Does each side fully intend to act as they say they will? Sometimes confusion exists between passive consensus, which is agreement to a course of action, and active consensus, where people are fully committed to carrying it out.

You must check that decisions are specific and understood. In a matter as crucial as a contract, you may even want to take legal advice. Make sure that actions are agreed by named individuals, and that you have clear procedures for follow-up.

In any meeting between cultures, the overwhelming danger is in reinforcing stereotypes. John Mole, in his entertaining book *Mind your Manners* (1995), says:

> Whether or not they exist in reality, stereotypes certainly exist in the perception of outsiders. And it is in perceptions of behaviour that misunderstandings occur. Avoiding them will make collaboration not necessarily more harmonious but at least more productive.

References

Bayne, R (1997) *The Myers-Briggs Type Indicator*, Nelson Thomas, London

Belbin, R M (1981) *Management Teams: Why they succeed or fail*, Heinemann, Oxford

de Bono, E (1982) *Lateral Thinking in Management*, Penguin, Harmondsworth

de Bono, E (1993) *Teach your Child to Think*, Penguin, Harmondsworth

Drucker, P (1979) *Management*, Pan Books, London

French, J R P and Raven, B H (1959) The bases of social power, in *Studies in Social Power*, ed D Cartwright, University of Michigan Press, Ann Arbor, MI

Gordon, W J J (1961) *Synectics*, Harper and Row, New York

Handy, C (1976) *Understanding Organizations*, Penguin, Harmondsworth

Janis, I L (1968) *Victims of Group Think: A psychological study of foreign policy decisions and fiascos*, Mifflin Houghton, Boston, MA

Jung, C G (1976) *The Portable Jung* (ed Joseph Campbell), Penguin, Harmondsworth

Kepner, C H and Tregoe, B B (1976) *The Rational Manager*, Kepner-Tregoe Inc, Princeton, NJ

Mole, J (1995) *Mind your Manners,* Nicholas Brealey, London
Osborn, A F (1963) *Applied Imagination*, Scribner, New York
Prince, G M (1970) *The Practice of Creativity*, Harper and Row, New York
Rickards, T (1990) *Creativity and Problem-solving at Work*, Gower, Aldershot
Senge, P (1993) *The Fifth Discipline*, Century Publishing, London
Tuckman, B (1965) Development sequences in small groups, *Psychological Bulletin*, **63**, pp 384–99